INVESTING
FOR
ETERNITY

BIBICAL PRINCIPLES
OF STEWARDSHIP

DR. DAVID JEREMIAH

with Dr. David Jeremiah

CONTENTS

ABOUT
DR. DAVID JEREMIAH
AND TURNING POINT

D r. David Jeremiah is the founder of Turning Point, a ministry committed to providing Christians with sound Bible teaching relevant to today's changing times through radio and television broadcasts, audio series, books, and rallies. Dr. Jeremiah's common-sense teaching on topics such as family, prayer, worship, angels, and biblical prophecy forms the foundation of Turning Point.

David and his wife, Donna, reside in El Cajon, California, where he serves as the senior pastor of Shadow Mountain Community Church. David and Donna have four children and ten grandchildren.

In 1982, Dr. Jeremiah brought the same solid teaching to San Diego television that he shares weekly with his congregation. Shortly thereafter, Turning Point expanded its ministry to radio. Dr. Jeremiah's inspiring messages can now be heard worldwide on radio, television, and the Internet.

Because Dr. Jeremiah desires to know his listening audience, he travels nationwide holding ministry rallies and spiritual enrichment conferences that touch the hearts and lives of many people. According to Dr. Jeremiah, "At some point in time, everyone reaches a turning point; and for every person, that moment is unique, an experience to hold onto forever. There's so much changing in today's world that sometimes it's difficult to choose the right path. Turning Point offers people an understanding of God's Word as well as the opportunity to make a difference in their lives."

Dr. Jeremiah has authored numerous books, including *Escape the Coming Night* (Revelation), *The Handwriting on the Wall* (Daniel), *Overcoming Loneliness, Grand Parenting, The Joy of Encouragement, Prayer—The Great Adventure, God in You* (Holy Spirit), *Gifts from God* (Parenting), *Jesus' Final Warning, When Your World Falls Apart, Slaying the Giants in Your Life, My Heart's Desire, Sanctuary, Searching for Heaven on Earth, The Secret of the Light, Captured by Grace, Discover Paradise, Grace Givers, Signs of Life, The 12 Ways of Christmas, 1 Minute a Day, What in the World Is Going On?, The Coming Economic Armageddon,* and *I Never Thought I'd See the Day!*

ABOUT THIS
STUDY GUIDE

The purpose of this Turning Point study guide is to reinforce Dr. David Jeremiah's dynamic, in-depth teaching and to aid the reader in applying biblical truth to his or her daily life. This study guide is designed to be used in conjunction with Dr. Jeremiah's *Investing for Eternity* audio series, but it may also be used by itself for personal or group study.

STRUCTURE OF THE LESSONS

Each lesson is based on one of the messages in the *Investing for Eternity* compact disc series and focuses on specific passages in the Bible. Each lesson is composed of the following elements:

- *Outline*

The outline at the beginning of the lesson gives a clear, concise picture of the topic being studied and provides a helpful framework for readers as they listen to Dr. Jeremiah's teaching.

- *Overview*

The overview summarizes Dr. Jeremiah's teaching on the passage being studied in the lesson. Readers should refer to the Scripture passages in their own Bibles as they study the overview. Unless otherwise indicated, Scripture verses quoted are taken from the New King James Version.

- *Application*

This section contains a variety of questions designed to help readers dig deeper into the lesson and the Scriptures, and to apply the lesson to their daily lives. For Bible study groups or Sunday school classes, these questions will provide a springboard for group discussion and interaction.

- *Did You Know?*

This section presents a fascinating fact, historical note, or insight that adds a point of interest to the preceding lesson.

Using This Guide for Group Study

The lessons in this study guide are suitable for Sunday school classes, small-group studies, elective Bible studies, or home Bible study groups. Each person in the group should have his or her own study guide.

When possible, the study guide should be used with the corresponding compact disc series. You may wish to assign the study guide lesson as homework prior to the meeting of the group and then use the meeting time to listen to the CD and discuss the lesson.

For Continuing Study

For a complete listing of Dr. Jeremiah's materials for personal and group study call 1-800-947-1993, go online to www.DavidJeremiah.org, or write to: Turning Point, P.O. Box 3838, San Diego, CA 92163.

Dr. Jeremiah's *Turning Point* program is currently heard or viewed around the world on radio, television, and the Internet in English. *Momento Decisivo,* the Spanish translation of Dr. Jeremiah's messages, can be heard on radio in every Spanish speaking country in the world. The television broadcast is also broadcast by satellite throughout the Middle East with Arabic subtitles.

Contact Turning Point for radio and television program times and stations in your area. Or visit our website at www.DavidJeremiah.org.

INVESTING FOR ETERNITY

INTRODUCTION

It has been said, "The way a man thinks about his money will determine the way he thinks about God." While that may be a stretch of the truth in light of Scripture, there is one thing that the Bible clearly teaches: The way a man thinks about God will determine the way he thinks about his money.

From cover to cover, the issue of material wealth is everywhere in the Bible. Lot's and Abraham's herdsmen quarreled because of an abundance of possessions. Esau "sold" his birthright for a mere bowl of stew. Joseph's brothers spared his life in order to gain a little profit. Moses disavowed great wealth to do what God called him to do. The Israelites plundered their Egyptian masters, then used that wealth to fashion a false god in the wilderness. God promised His people the wealth of the land of Canaan, but then allowed them to suffer defeat when one person kept plunder that was under His ban. Ruth and Naomi had not a penny to their names, but found favor from God through a wealthy man named Boaz. David went from rags to riches, while Solomon went from wealth to utter despair. The Pharisees craved wealth, while the Son of Man had nowhere to lay His head. Ananias and Sapphira lied and died over giving their money to the church, while the Macedonians gave until it hurt. And while we may or may not feel we have enough to live on today, God promises that one day we will walk with solid gold under our feet.

So how are we to think about money—and about our God-given stewardship of it—right here, right now, as believers? The media loves to paint a caricature of Christian leaders with one hand on the Bible and the other in our pockets, but does that absolve us of our responsibility to give to God by giving to His work? The rule in the working world today is that "time is money," but does that mean I can give of my time and not my money? The Old Testament established the rule of the tithe, but as a New Testament believer, can I cheat that down so it doesn't hurt so much?

While many churches and ministries today have turned to human effort and clever schemes to meet the "bottom line," the Bible offers a better way, and that is the focus of this crucial series. Call it "stewardship," "giving," "tithing," "gifts and offerings," or whatever you will. It's as much a part of the Christian life as prayer, witnessing, and Bible study; and, as such, it deserves to be addressed.

Of course, it's obvious that this is no simple issue. But in this study Dr. Jeremiah offers clear, simple, biblical answers which consistently show that God's plan for our money is to benefit us, benefit His people, benefit His work, and benefit Him, all at the same time! In 10 concise lessons, Dr. Jeremiah allows God's Word to challenge us to turn over to Christ an area of our lives that may be the last to bow the knee to His lordship—though certainly not the least important.

With Bible in hand, Dr. Jeremiah carefully examines issues of tithing, organized giving, God's "portfolios," personal stewardship, genuine commitment motivated by faith, and some truly Solomonic advice about wealth and one's relationship with God. He surveys a multitude of Scriptures that address the issue of money in general and about giving specifically. He takes a fresh look at the principle of "sowing and reaping" as well as the vital connection between God's grace and "grace giving."

In short, for those who want to get to the bottom of perhaps the thorniest issue of our times, this study in God's Word will provide answers that we not only can live with, but can't live without.

PUTTING GOD FIRST IN OUR LIVES

Deuteronomy 26, 1 Kings 17

In this lesson we observe the amazing principle of giving first to God, even when it defies all logic and our very survival.

OUTLINE

When Elijah first approached the widow of Sidon, there was no way she could have foreseen the way God would meet her pressing need for food. Yet she took God at His word, put Him first above all—and that's when the truly miraculous began to happen.

   I.   **When We Put God First and Tithe, We Possess Our Possessions**

  II. **When We Put God First and Tithe, We Prepare for the Future**

 III. **When We Put God First and Tithe, We Place Faith Over Sight**

 IV. **When We Put God First and Tithe, We Put Him to Work on Our Behalf**

OVERVIEW

God has instituted some very practical ways to help us keep Him first in our lives. In the Old Testament, God desired to be first in the lives of His people, so all of the feasts and sacrifices in some way pointed to the priority of putting Him first in their lives.

In fact, the Bible says God is a jealous God and won't share His honor and glory with anyone. One of the early feasts was the Feast of Firstfruits which was the practice of first fruit giving. Listen to the words of the Lord to His people to help them keep Him number one in their lives:

> "And it shall be, when you come into the land which the Lord your God is giving you as an inheritance, and you possess it and dwell in it, that you shall take some of the first of all the produce of the ground, which you shall bring from your land that the Lord your God is giving you, and put it in a basket and go to the place where the Lord your God chooses to make His name abide. And you shall go to the one who is priest in those days, and say to him, 'I declare today to the Lord your God that I have come to the country which the Lord swore to our fathers to give us.' Then the priest shall take the basket out of your hand and set it down before the altar of the Lord your God. . . . Then you shall set it before the Lord your God, and worship before the Lord your God" (Deuteronomy 26:1–4, 10b).

God told His people that when they began to enjoy all the good things He promised, they were to offer Him the first fruits of that goodness. By doing that they would be saying, "I am putting You first in my life; and I am being reminded that everything I have comes from You, and I'm bringing back the firstfruits of this offering and giving it to You as a sacrifice to my God."

As long as the Jewish people did that, God blessed them. When they stopped doing that, they fell into awful sin and decay. I think it is like that for most of us. When we put God first in our lives, God blesses us. And when we cease to put Him first, we experience the consequences.

A story in 1 Kings 17, involving the prophet Elijah, illustrates this principle of first things first. We need to set the context in order to understand what happened.

God had sent word to His people through Elijah that no rain was forthcoming. Then God told Elijah to go eastward and hide by the Brook Cherith. There God provided drink from the brook and bread and meat from the ravens.

God didn't forget His prophet Elijah in the face of draught. He took care of him by the Brook Cherith; then, when the brook dried up and Elijah didn't know what to do, God gave him specific instruction. God spoke to him and said, "I have some instruction for you. Here is how I am going to take care of you now."

What God told Elijah to do was about as illogical as anything could have been. We read in 1 Kings 17:8 these words: "Then the word of the Lord came to him, saying, 'Arise, go to Zarephath, which belongs to Sidon, and dwell there. See, I have commanded a widow there to provide for you.'"

Once we understand the background of this story, it is truly astounding. Sidon was a hundred miles from Elijah, and there was famine in the land. Also, Sidon was a Phoenician city that was the center of Baal worship. So, God was telling Elijah "Go to the center of Baal worship in Sidon, and I'm going to care for you there." To Elijah this made no sense at all. Later, in 1 Kings 18:19–40, we read another story about how God cared for Elijah in the center of Baal worship. God gave Elijah a marvelous moment of victory on Mount Carmel. Elijah had challenged the prophets of Baal and won. In fact, Elijah had all the prophets of Baal killed, thus enraging King Ahab and his wife, Jezebel.

Once Elijah arrived in Zarephath in 1 Kings 17, God's instructions seemed even more illogical. We read in verses 10–12:

> So he arose and went to Zarephath. And when he came to the gate of the city, indeed a widow was there gathering sticks. And he called to her and said, "Please bring me a little water in a cup, that I may drink." And as she was going to get it, he called to her and said, "Please bring me a morsel of bread in your hand." So she said, "As the Lord your God lives, I do not have bread, only a handful of flour in a bin, and a little oil in a jar; and see, I am gathering a couple of sticks that I may go in and prepare it for myself and my son, that we may eat it, and die.

I wonder what was going through Elijah's mind about this time. Perhaps it was, "This is how God is going to care for me?"

But notice what he said in verse 13: "And Elijah said to her, 'Do not fear; go and do as you have said, but make me a small cake from it first, and bring it to me; and afterward make some for yourself and your son.'"

The widow must have been wondering what was going on. She had just explained to Elijah that she had nothing left. Her flour barrel was dry; she had just a tiny bit of oil left in her jar. She was going to make one last meal for herself and her son, and then die. But Elijah said, "Make me a cake first."

That's the way some feel about giving to God. We have bills and responsibilities, but then someone says, "Put God first." That's when we may think, "That is the most illogical thing I've ever heard in my life."

If we read the story of the widow carefully, we learn some very encouraging things.

WHEN WE PUT GOD FIRST AND TITHE, WE POSSESS OUR POSSESSIONS

When Elijah met the widow of Zarephath, she was locked in the clutches of a handful of meal and a tiny bit of oil. That's all she had. We can sympathize with her. In fact, some of us can identify with her. And Elijah's heart went out to her. But the difference was that he knew something she didn't know. He knew that the way to have what you have and have it to the fullest is always to put God first. That's why he said, "Make me a little cake first." In other words, "Trust God by putting Him first and watch what He does."

When we first see the widow in this story, she is clutching everything she has. At the end of the story, she is releasing it all to God. The way to have what you have is to give it back to God. That is the only way you can ever possess your possessions. If you clutch them to yourself, the only thing you will ever have is what you hold in your hands. But if you give it back to God with open hands, He will not only bless you, He can also put back what you need. This is the principle of the open hand.

WHEN WE PUT GOD FIRST AND TITHE, WE PREPARE FOR THE FUTURE

Before the widow gave the first cake to Elijah, she was preparing to die. She said, "This is it." How bleak was the outlook for this

woman! But when she left the future in the hands of God and gave what she could to God, He took care of her.

Some may say, "I can't afford to tithe. If I didn't have to worry about this and I didn't have to worry about that, and if we didn't have this and that, or if we only had more money, then we could do it." But the fact is that the acquisition of more goods does not diminish fear—it multiplies it.

When we put God first and give Him what is rightfully His, we can quit worrying about the future. God will take care of us. He will never be in debt to somebody who puts Him first.

WHEN WE PUT GOD FIRST AND TITHE, WE PLACE FAITH OVER SIGHT

The Bible says that as Christians we are to walk by faith and not by sight. I've never met anyone who started to tithe because it looked like a good thing to do or because it made sense to do it. The only way you will ever do it is to respond to what God has said in His book and say, "God said it, I believe it, and that settles it." That's what the widow had to do.

The only thing Elijah said to her was, "Make me a little cake first." That's all the word she had. She could have reasoned, "Let me see if I have enough for myself and my son first. Then I'll respond." Or, "Let me see how things go first, and let me see if I can do that for you."

But verse 15 says, "So she went away and did according to the word of Elijah." She understood that Elijah was speaking from God, and she did what God told her to do—not because it made sense, but because God said it.

If you are trying to figure out what is the right time to begin to tithe based upon where you are and thinking things through in your family economy, it will never happen. The truth is that God has said we should tithe; and we respond by faith, not by sight.

WHEN WE PUT GOD FIRST AND TITHE, WE PUT HIM TO WORK ON OUR BEHALF

Notice 1 Kings 17, verses 14–15: "For thus says the Lord God of Israel: 'The bin of flour shall not be used up, nor shall the jar of oil run dry, until the day the Lord sends rain on the earth.' So she went away and did according to the word of Elijah; and she and he and her household ate for many days."

God spoke, she responded, and the fulfillment of the promise was sure. God did exactly what He said He was going to do.

It is not hard to imagine the joy in this lady's household as every day she went to the pantry to look in the barrel, and every day there was enough to sustain the three of them for one more day. Just 24 hours worth of flour and oil—and the next day she went back and it was replenished again.

Because she had also allowed the prophet to stay in her home, the widow had the added blessing of this man of God praying for her and her family. By faith, the widow put God first, and God blessed her and met every one of her needs. That's what God has promised to do for anyone who will put Him first in their lives.

Many Christians who have been experiencing this with the Lord over years of tithing and first fruits giving can give testimony of how God has worked on their behalf. It is often illogical, and often incredible, to see God work at the moment of an unexpected need. He is never going to be in debt to any of His people who put Him first.

In Matthew 6:33 Jesus said, "But seek first the kingdom of God and His righteousness, and all these things shall be added to you." Don't wait until everything else is exhausted. Put Him in the number one position in your life.

This widow had a promise from God, and she followed through. She took the orders as they were given to her, and she put God first. As a result, God met every need in her life. She was a wealthy woman because she put God first.

Some years back I heard on the news about a woman who lived in West Palm Beach, Florida. She had died at the age of seventy-one all alone in her apartment. The coroner's report cited the cause of death as malnutrition. By the time she died, she had wasted away to 50 pounds. And when investigators found her, the place she lived in was a virtual pig pen—the most unbelievable mess they had ever seen. As they continued their investigation, they found out she had begged food at her neighbor's back door. She had obtained the few clothes she had from the Salvation Army. And from all outward appearances, she was a penniless recluse, a pitiful and forgotten widow.

But as they dug through her apartment, they found among the debris of her unclaimed and shambled belongings two keys. Those keys led officials to safe deposit boxes at two different local banks. And what they found there was absolutely incredible.

The first safe deposit box contained seven hundred stock certificates, plus hundreds of other valuable certificates and bonds and solid financial securities, not to mention a stack of cash amounting to nearly $200,000! The second box had no certificates, but held $600,000 in cash. Adding up the net worth of both safe deposit boxes, investigators found that the woman possessed well over a million dollars.

In other words, she was a millionaire who died a victim of starvation in an impoverished home all by herself.

Many of God's people live in the spiritual, as well as the financial, realm far below the level where God wants them to live simply because they haven't trusted Him totally. God's written Word should be enough to motivate us to take Him at His word and begin to live the way He has called us to live.

APPLICATION

1. Concerning the person to whom Elijah was sent, read Deuteronomy 28:1, 8–10, 15 and 24, and answer these questions:

   a. Why do you think God sent Elijah to a widow in a foreign country?

   b. Whose benefit do you think God had in mind?

   c. In light of what later happened on Mt. Carmel, what kind of object lesson might this have been for the people of Israel?

2. Read Hebrews 11:1. How does this relate to the widow's actions in this episode?

   a. What, ultimately, was the widow willing to do in order to do first what God had told her to do?

3. What, in light of the following passages, is God's concept of putting Him first?

   Luke 21:2–4

Luke 6:38

Nehemiah 10:37

2 Chronicles 31:4–5

4. Seeking God is first contrasted to what in Matthew 6:25, 32–33?

5. Read Matthew 10:39, 16:25–26. How is the principle of "possessing what you possess" by first giving it to God reflected in the nature of salvation in Christ?

   a. Can you make a logical connection between the two?

6. Read Philippians 4:19.

   a. How might Christians understand this verse if it were not written within its historical context?

b. Now read the preceding verses, 4:15–18. What were the precise circumstances to which Paul was referring?

c. What Old Testament principle is Paul applying here?

d. How might that apply to us today?

DID YOU KNOW?

The entire issue of Baal worship—concerning which God called Elijah as a prophet of God's truth—revolved around the question of whether the God of Israel could provide for His people if they merely obeyed Him. In the land of Israel, there was no river system that provided the water necessary for a fruitful harvest. God had said that if His people would obey Him, including the offering of firstfruits from the land, He would faithfully provide the rain from season to season. If, however, they became disobedient, He would withhold the rain in order to call them to repentance.

That's where Israel thought they found an "out." Baal—the Canaanite god of storms—could provide the rain that God withheld (or so they thought). That way they could have their sin and the rain, too. But, as the episode with Elijah and the prophets of Baal shows, they were gravely mistaken. God alone controls the blessing of fruitfulness, and no amount of wishful thinking (or Baal worship) changes His requirements of obedience.

GIVING YOURSELF FIRST TO GOD

2 Corinthians 8

This lesson focuses on the most important issue in giving, first giving one's life to God without reservation.

OUTLINE

When Paul wrote to the Corinthians about the principle of selfless giving, there was no better example he could hold up than the churches in Macedonia. However, their giving was not a matter of skimming something off an abundance of wealth. Theirs was a sacrificial giving that had begun with an initial total commitment to Christ.

What, then, will that kind of commitment consist of?

I.   **We Realize That Everything Belongs to God in the First Place**

II. **We Respond to God by Willingly Giving of Our Substance**

III. **We Recognize Our Own Personal Accountability to God**

IV. **We Release Back to God That Which We Know Is His Anyway**

V.   **We Regularly Give of Our Substance**

VI. **We Receive His Guaranteed Promise of Supply**

W

e begin this lesson by looking at 2 Corinthians 8:1–5:

"Moreover, brethren, we make known to you the grace of
God bestowed on the churches of Macedonia: that in a
great trial of affliction the abundance of their joy and their
deep poverty abounded in the riches of their liberality.
For I bear witness that according to their ability, yes, and
beyond their ability, they were freely willing, imploring us
with much urgency that we would receive the gift and the
fellowship of the ministering to the saints. And not only as
we had hoped, but *they first gave themselves to the Lord, and
then to us by the will of God.*"

The three churches of Macedonia to which Paul refers in
2 Corinthians 8 and 9 are discussed in Acts 16 and 17, and they
are churches about which we have some information. They are
the church at Philippi, the church at Thessalonica, and the church
of Berea. And if we study the book of Acts and read the letters of
Paul to Philippi and Thessalonica, we learn the characteristics
which made these Macedonian people abound to every good work.

In 2 Corinthians 8 and 9, Paul writes to the Corinthians and
teaches them about the grace of giving. In so doing, he uses the
Macedonians as an example of how to give in a time of affliction
and poverty. The Macedonians were a very poor people. They did
not have much to offer. And no doubt they went through all of the
challenging questions that present themselves to us today when
we are confronted with the opportunity of giving to God. Will they
have enough left over if they give to God first? If they participate
in an offering for the poor saints, will they be able to meet their
own needs?

But, as Paul points out, what was truly amazing about the
Macedonian offering was not how much they gave, but the fact
that before they gave anything, they first gave themselves to God.
And that's the point of this lesson: first things first.

The Bible teaches that it is very difficult to become a good
steward, a faithful giver to God, if we haven't first given ourselves

to Him. There is an undeniable principle that if God owns me—if I have given myself to Him by way of dedication—then whatever I have and whatever resources are available to me all belong to God. This is far removed from and far above the superficial issue of wrenching a tithe out of an unwilling giver on a periodic basis at church on Sunday.

The background of this passage is that the Macedonians had come to a place of commitment and dedication where they said, "We belong to God, and we are going to give ourselves back to Him again in dedication." Once they did that, the rest was easy.

Romans 12:1 admonishes us to "present your bodies a living sacrifice, holy, acceptable to God, which is your reasonable service." God is far more interested in the giver than He is in the gift. He cares a lot more about what happens to us in the process of giving than whether or not we give money to Him. The fact is that God doesn't really need our money. His resources are limitless. The whole issue of giving is what it does in our lives and how it prepares us regularly to reflect our obedience and love for God. And because God is more interested in the giver than in the gift, the importance of total consecration cannot be overemphasized.

Sometimes we think, "God has most of my life." There are many wonderful Christians, people who serve and teach, people who read their Bibles every day, but this matter of giving to God has escaped them—or perhaps they have escaped it. They have just never come to grips with it.

For any Christian, one area of life not given back to God will drive them to distraction throughout their Christian life. It's as though they can never feel like they have total victory because they've never come to the place where they've said, "Lord, I want to give myself to You—whatever that entails, whatever that involves." But when we do that, when we give ourselves first to God, as the Macedonians did, then everything else starts to fall into place.

As we study this matter of giving to God, we need to realize that our first commitment is to give ourselves to God. First and foremost, if you have never personally trusted Christ as your Savior, if you have never really humbled yourself before God, acknowledged your sin and asked Jesus Christ to give you freedom and forgiveness, that's where any kind of stewardship commitment has to start. You must give yourself to Him first.

If you are a Christian but you have been holding back a part of your life, you will never really have the joy that you desire as a Christian until you give yourself first to God.

Remember: The Macedonians gave first of themselves to God, then they gave their offering. So we need to examine what that means and what that might look like for us.

WE REALIZE THAT EVERYTHING BELONGS TO GOD IN THE FIRST PLACE

The Macedonians gave themselves to God first. As we read in 2 Corinthians 8:5, "Not only as we had hoped, but they first gave themselves to the Lord, and then to us by the will of God." It became easy for the Macedonians to give because when they gave themselves to God, they understood that they really always belonged to God in the first place.

In Ezekiel 18:4, God says it this way: "Behold, all souls are Mine; the soul of the father as well as the soul of the son is Mine." God owns everything, including us; and acknowledging that ownership in our lives is what sets us free to be who God wants us to be. If we live or if we die, according to the New Testament, we do it unto the Lord. "Therefore, whether we live or die, we are the Lord's" (Romans 14:8).

First Corinthians 6:19–20 tells us, "Do you not know that your body is the temple of the Holy Spirit who is in you, whom you have from God, and you are not your own? For you were bought at a price; therefore glorify God in your body and in your spirit, which are God's."

The New Testament clearly teaches that we belong to God. When we acknowledge that, we are simply acknowledging something that is already true. God owns it all, whatever resources we have. For some that is quite an amount; for others, it is not very much. But whatever we have, it belongs to God.

So when we come to God and say, "God, I really do understand that I belong to You, and that all I have belongs to You," it takes all the pressure off of the tug-of-war that goes on between churches and people in regard to the giving of their money to the Lord.

WE RESPOND TO GOD BY WILLINGLY GIVING OF OUR SUBSTANCE

Giving is no longer a matter of reluctance, but something we want to do. Second Corinthians 9:7 says, "So let each one give as he purposes in his heart, not grudgingly or of necessity; for God loves a cheerful giver." If you have given yourself to God, you will never have a problem with your attitude in giving your resources to God. You will give with joy in your heart, with great excitement that you can be a part of His ministry.

But if you are holding out on God, you will always struggle with this issue. Your giving is a good barometer to check, to see how you are doing in your commitment to Christ.

WE RECOGNIZE OUR OWN PERSONAL ACCOUNTABILITY TO GOD

There is a rumor afoot that God holds churches accountable for how much they give. But that's all it is—a rumor. That's not the truth. In no place does the Bible even hint that God holds a church accountable for its giving. However, God does operate on an individual accountability basis. And that's very clear in Scripture.

When we give ourselves to God first, we understand that we are accountable to Him as His people. The Bible says we are to lay by each week that which God has entrusted to us (1 Corinthians 16:2). And we are reminded over and over in the New Testament that someday we are to give an account to God for what we have done.

If I have given myself to God first, if I have said, "God, everything that I am, everything that I have belongs to You," then I don't really have to live in fear of that day of accountability. I've already had my day of accountability. I've stood before God the best I know how and said, "God, You direct me, and I'll be a funnel for whatever You put in my hands. I am going to be accountable to You as You tell me in Your Word what You want me to be."

That may be one of the reasons why many Christians fear the idea of stewardship—because down deep in their hearts they are aware of their accountability before God. One of these days, God is going to give us the opportunity to give an account of all of the resources He has put within our hands from the beginning of our Christian experience until the day we are no longer able to manage on this earth. And that can be a scary thought.

However, if you give yourself first to God, then all the rest of it falls into place.

WE RELEASE BACK TO GOD THAT WHICH WE KNOW IS HIS ANYWAY

When the first issue is settled, then we're not saying to God, "Lord, I'll give You some of my money." When you know that you are God's, and all you have is God's, you can say, "God, how much of what You've entrusted to me do I need to keep for myself, and how much should I return to the kingdom's work so that You can do what needs to be done here on this earth?" The Bible tells us we are to do this in a regular, systematic way on the first day of the week.

WE REGULARLY GIVE OF OUR SUBSTANCE

When I give myself to God, then I get into a pattern, even a habit. In the New Testament, we're told to do this on the first day of the week (1 Corinthians 16:2). That's how we're to operate as Christians. It doesn't mean that when I give myself to God I just sort of randomly respond here and there. Rather, because God is a systematic God, He has a systematic plan so His work can go forward.

WE RECEIVE HIS GUARANTEED PROMISE OF SUPPLY

In Philippians 4, Paul is talking about an offering that was taken for him. The Philippians had done a wonderful thing, so Paul is thanking them for giving to him in such a generous way. As he concludes his thanksgiving and talks about all the goodness that happened because they had given, he ends his letter with this promise in the nineteenth verse: "My God shall supply all your need according to His riches in glory by Christ Jesus."

That promise is in the context of those who have put God first in their lives. What Paul is saying is this: You will never have to worry about your need being met if you give yourself first to God. He has obligated Himself to meet the need in your life. When we give ourselves to God first, we receive His guaranteed promise of supply.

Does that mean that we will always have everything we want? No. Some of the things we want we shouldn't have, and God is not going to supply them. Does that mean I'm going to be the richest person in town? No. It means exactly what it says:

"My God shall supply all your need according to His riches in glory by Christ Jesus."

If we refuse to put God first in our giving, we are in effect saying, "I don't believe that God tells the truth. I don't believe God can do what He says He will do."

As we study this whole matter of stewardship, we must realize that giving isn't just a financial decision. Stewardship gets right to the center of whether or not we have truly committed ourselves totally to Jesus Christ. It's easy to say with our lips where we are, but when we get down to the substance of our lives, we will know what we really believe in.

First things first. Let's make sure that first we have given ourselves to God.

1. What do the following passages reveal about God's ownership of all things, and the expected response to that fact?

   Exodus 9:29

   Exodus 19:5

   Job 41:11

   Psalm 24:1

   Psalm 50:10–12

2. Describe in one sentence what you perceive to be the world system's view of personal wealth and possessions.

   a. Now describe what you perceive to be the popular Christian view in comparison to the world's.

   b. Do you think it is a positive view? Why or why not?

3. Think of a parallel in everyday life to the concept of giving yourself and all you are first, then giving from what is yours.

a. Does this match the biblical concept? Why or why not?

4. Read 1 Timothy 6:5–11, and then consider:

   a. What connection do the "corrupt" make between godliness and wealth in verse 5?

   b. What does Paul describe as "great gain" in verse 6?

   c. What is his line of reasoning? Is he thinking of a principle that isn't stated here? What might that be?

d. What is his measure of material "gain"?

e. In verse 9, what is the point of departure from spiritual gain?

f. What is the parallel statement in verse 10?

g. What is the response of the already-committed believer to be in the face of this attitude (verse 11)?

5. Returning to Romans 12:1, how might you paraphrase this verse to emphasize the point of this lesson?

DID YOU KNOW?

C hurch history seems to indicate that the first century Christians who were so faithful to supply the needs of their persecuted brethren did so over and above the level of giving prescribed by Jewish law. Why? Because they frequently heard about their Christian brothers and sisters who were suffering materially because of persecution at the hands of the Romans as well as some Jewish leaders. But then they knew their faithfulness to give to God in the way recognized by the Old Testament was essential to their witness before their fellow Jews whom they longed to see come to faith in Jesus as Messiah.

Their solution? Give from their resources, however limited, so the work of the Gospel might continue unhindered as God chose to bless. Apparently, their last thought was for their own material comfort.

STEWARDSHIP IS LORDSHIP

Colossians 1:15–19

In this lesson the supreme position of Jesus Christ as Lord of creation as well as Lord of the church is shown to be the basis for His lordship over the Christian in the matter of stewardship.

OUTLINE

The Colossians of Paul's day faced a dilemma not unlike our own: How important is it that we, as believers, acknowledge Christ's supreme position over all things? After all, if He is ultimately Lord of all, then it follows that He must be Lord over my life. In this series, we might well ask how that may impact not only our stewardship for Christ, but our obedience in every area.

   I.   **Jesus Christ, The Lord of Creation**

  II.   **Jesus Christ, The Goal of Creation**

 III.   **Jesus Christ, The Sustainer of Creation**

 IV.   **Jesus Christ, The Lord of the Church**

I sn't it true that for most of us we consult the Lord as a last resort, having tried everything else? And then, when we ask Him to help us, if He gives us instructions that are difficult for us to obey, we don't like to hear those words. So we ask, "Lord, can You give me something easier to do?"

Our modern concept of the lordship of Jesus Christ may best be summarized by Peter's confusing statement in some translations of Acts 10:14, where he responded to the Lord by saying, "Not so, Lord!" If we say, "Not so" to Christ, then He isn't Lord. And if He is Lord, we do not say to Him, "Not so."

In Luke 6:46 Jesus said to His friends, "Why do you call Me 'Lord, Lord,' and not do the things which I say?" It was an incongruous thought in the mind of our Lord that anyone could say, "Lord," and then not do what He tells him to do.

In the days of the Roman empire everyone was required to put a pinch of incense on the altar and confess, "Caesar is Lord." And because the Christians would not do this, many of them died a martyr's death. Believers in that day were clear in their minds about the "lordship" of Jesus Christ. They knew that allegiance to their Lord demanded renunciation of all other lords. To them, lordship was the ultimate issue. And today, if we are to have the impact on our generation that they had on theirs, we need to get back to His lordship as the ultimate issue of our lives as well.

If the lordship of Christ is resolved in our hearts, then all of the other questions become incidental.

When we say that Jesus Christ is Lord, we mean there can be no limitations to that issue. If He is Lord, He rules every creature and everything everywhere. He is Lord in heaven; He is Lord over all the worlds; He is Lord over the angels; and He is Lord over Satan and all the powers of darkness. He is Lord of His church; He is Lord over all the nations; He is Lord over all things animate and inanimate. He is Lord over everything—and He ought to be Lord over us.

This one issue divides the world perhaps more than any other. People always take sides when it comes to the lordship of Jesus Christ. Even now in the evangelical world, there is a war over the concept of the lordship of Jesus Christ—not just between those who believe and those who do not believe, but among those who believe.

Most people in the world will not argue over whether or not there is a supernatural being. But when you talk about a Savior who is Christ the Lord, they resist. But the New Testament tells us that Jesus is the One to whom all authority has been given. He is the One on whom the Father looked and was pleased, and when we present Jesus Christ as Lord, people always take sides.

The New Testament passage which presents Jesus as Lord perhaps better than any other we might choose is Colossians 1:15–19:

He is the image of the invisible God, the firstborn over all creation. For by Him all things were created that are in heaven and that are on earth, visible and invisible, whether thrones or dominions or principalities or powers. All things were created through Him and for Him. And He is before all things, and in Him all things consist. And He is the head of the body, the church, who is the beginning, the firstborn from the dead, that in all things He may have the preeminence. For it pleased the Father that in Him all the fullness should dwell.

Paul wrote these words to the Colossian church because false teaching had begun to creep in among these believers. The specific kind of false teaching relegated Jesus Christ to a position of unimportance. This teaching stated that God was up there, and that from God there were eons that emanated out from Him like concentric circles, until finally you got down to man, so that man was sort of a projection from God. Somewhere among those circles between God the Creator and man the created was Jesus Christ— a created being of God.

They did not deny that Christ was Christ, but they did not give Him the supreme place of ultimate importance that the Word of God accords Him. So the Colossians were not much different than the average Christian today who wants to make Jesus Christ "Lord," wants to make a deep commitment to Him, and yet at the same time wants to enjoy everything else that is in the world. They don't mind having Christ as long as He is not supreme. They don't mind having Him as their Savior as long as He doesn't have to be their Lord. And if they can fit Him comfortably with every other thing that is going on in their lives, then it is wonderfully convenient to be a Christian.

But when you talk to a Christian today about making Jesus Christ Lord of his life, you have drawn that line again. And you have created an issue in his life. Paul had a number of options open to him as he tried to combat the heresy in the Colossian church. He could have done as modern apologists do, taken all of the tenets of their faith, and one by one taken them apart. But Paul, as he wrote to the Colossians, thought the best message he could preach was that of presenting Jesus Christ in all of His glory, majesty, power, and greatness.

So he undertakes in the first few verses of Colossians to lift up Jesus and present Him as He truly is. He points to Jesus as the central figure in history. He says of Jesus Christ that He is preeminent. He speaks of Him as the Creator God. He knows that if he can get the Colossians to come to grips with who Christ is and what He has done, they would get rid of the false teaching that was poisoning their church. So he presents Jesus Christ as Lord.

JESUS CHRIST, THE LORD OF CREATION

Jesus Christ, said Paul, is the Lord of creation. That's the logical starting place for any presentation of the lordship of Jesus Christ. The Colossian heresy taught that Jesus Christ was a created being. But Paul presented Him as the very agent of creation Himself. He said, "By Him all things were created that are in heaven and that are on earth, visible and invisible" (Colossians 1:16).

JESUS CHRIST, THE GOAL OF CREATION

And He is also the goal of creation. "For all things were created . . . for Him," said Paul in verse 16. And as the agent and goal of creation, Jesus Christ is also the sustainer of creation.

JESUS CHRIST, THE SUSTAINER OF CREATION

Paul writes that "in Him all things consist" (verse 17), or hold together. Paul is saying that Jesus Christ is not a created being. He is the One who has created the world that we see and know. Not only did He create it, but the whole world was created for Him. He is the agent and the goal of creation; and not only is He the agent and goal of creation, He is the sustaining influence that holds creation together.

That means that if for one moment the Lord Jesus Christ would withdraw His sustaining hand from the universe as you and I know it, it would fly off into oblivion and be destroyed. Jesus Christ is the Creator, the Sustainer, and the Goal of the world as we know it. He is the Lord of creation, the fundamental principle of the universe.

No wonder the humanists and those who like to level their heavy artillery at the Christian church choose to make the creationist view their point of attack. Is it because they are interested in settling the issue of the origin of the universe? Actually, that is very far down on their list of concerns. The real issue in the mind of the secular humanists—the reason they go against the creationists as they do—is because they know that if Jesus Christ is Lord of creation, then He is the One who holds claim over their lives. The issue is who is to control one's life. And if Jesus Christ is Lord of the universe, then He has every right to be Lord of the lives of those He has created.

As we study in the gospel of John the life and ministry of the Lord Jesus Christ, it becomes evident to us that Jesus was sovereign over creation when He chose to be, even as the incarnate Son of God. He demonstrated His absolute sovereignty and lordship over His creation. He spoke and the wind and the sea obeyed Him. At His command, the properties of water changed into new wine. The lame and the blind and the infirm came to Him, He spoke, and their degenerate limbs and body instruments were restored to new life. In His resurrection body, He was not bound by time and space as we are. And His ultimate triumph over death and the grave settled forever His right to rule over the universe. Jesus Christ is Lord! He is Lord of His creation.

JESUS CHRIST, THE LORD OF THE CHURCH

Verses 17–18 tell us, "He is before all things, and in Him all things consist. And He is the head of the body, the church." Not only is He Lord of creation, He is Lord of the church. And this passage presents Him as the head of the body. The New Testament pictures the church as a body on earth which is controlled by the head which is in heaven. Just as a human body gets its signals from the head, the body which is the church living here on this earth gets its signals from Jesus Christ who is the head.

Paul is saying that just as Christ is the Lord of creation, He is also Lord of the church. In verse 17 he uses the term, "before all things," and then in verse 18 he says that "in all things He may have the preeminence." In other words, Paul is saying Christ is already sovereign over the first creation by virtue of His work, and now He desires to be sovereign over His creation, the church.

Perhaps that explains to us the coldness and deadness of the church today. Is it possible that the church is a body separated from its head? The Colossians had fallen into this pit. They lost the focus of Jesus Christ in their lives. They had replaced the Lord Jesus Christ with visions and angel worship and human traditions and asceticism, and they were in danger of losing all of their power. Why? Because they had cut themselves off from the head. They were like a disembodied individual, walking around without any strength, without any direction, without any signals.

So Paul writes back to them and he says, "Just as the Lord is Lord of Creation, He is the Lord of the church; and if you want the blessing of Jesus Christ in your life, you better plug into the head because that is where the source of strength is. That's where the direction comes from."

If Jesus Christ is the head of the church, He must have sovereign control over the church. Trustees serve under Christ. Deacons serve under Christ. The Word is preached in Him and under Him and before Him. The whole church unites with Peter and Paul and the entire Christian community in confirming that He is Lord of all (Acts 10:36).

As you trust God in regard to stewardship, don't do what you think you can do. Ask God to tell you what He wants you to do. Make sure there is a measure of faith in it. Make sure there is sacrifice in it. Because if there is not, it will leave you with an empty feeling. Ask God to show you what He wants you to do.

1. What attributes of Jesus Christ can be seen in the following passages, and how might each one affect our practice of stewardship?

   1 Corinthians 3:11–13

   Ephesians 1:22–23

   Colossians 3:1

   Hebrews 5:8

2. What is Christ's relationship to the creation, according to:

John 1:1–3

Luke 6:5

Matthew 9:5–6

Mark 4:39–40

3. Based on the above verses, why might we, as believers, be motivated to express our belief in His lordship through stewardship?

4. What relationship might there be between 1 Peter 3:22, which indicates the present location of Jesus Christ in His resurrection body, and Luke 12:33–34?

   a. How might this affect our view of giving?

5. According to Philippians 4:10–17, to whose ultimate benefit did Paul view the gift he received?

   a. What would this tell us about God's purpose in using believers to help meet the needs of other believers?

6. What does Ephesians 6:7–8 apparently reveal about the relationship between one's view of the lordship of Christ and one's charity toward others?

a. How might this translate into a biblical attitude toward stewardship and giving?

DID YOU KNOW?

One vivid picture of the irony and futility of attempting to hold onto wealth no matter what befalls us is provided by the history of the community at Qumran—the Jewish sect that hid away what is known today as the Dead Sea Scrolls. In addition to hiding multiple copies of the Scriptures as their Roman persecutors threatened them, they also were apparently quite concerned about preserving the wealth that had been turned over to the ascetic community by those who joined them. So they carefully catalogued each cache of coins and precious metals, hid them, and then recorded the hiding places as well—on a scroll of copper that would survive all processes of decay.

As it turns out, over the 2,000 years from then until the scroll was discovered, all the landmarks necessary for recovering the wealth perished or were covered over. All that was found in the caves at Qumran were the "perishable" scrolls of the Word of God, and the copper scroll. The treasure itself was apparently lost forever.

SOLOMON'S ADVICE ABOUT MONEY

Selected Scriptures

In this lesson we listen to perhaps the wisest consultant of all time concerning money—King Solomon himself.

OUTLINE

If there's one person in history who has known both the highest highs and the lowest lows related to money, it is King Solomon of Israel. And though his once godly life apparently took a turn for the worse as the years wore on, his wisdom concerning the basics of life—even money—did not abandon him. So it is to his records of wisdom that we look for financial advice.

I. **Risky Assumptions**
    A. Money Brings Satisfaction
    B. Money Brings Significance
    C. Money Brings Security

II. **Right Attitudes**
    A. Money Is a Gift From God
    B. Money Is to Be Enjoyed

III. **Righteous Actions**
    A. Tithing Is God's Way of Perpetuating His Program
    B. Tithing Is God's Way of Pointing Out Our Priorities
    C. Tithing Is God's Way of Proving God's Promises
    D. Tithing Is God's Way of Promoting Our Faith
    E. Tithing Is God's Way of Providing for Our Needs

OVERVIEW

There are few, if any, things in the Christian life that cause people more anxiety, more stress, more disagreement than the whole issue of money.

Money is who we are, it is what we do, it is our very life, our very self. So when we deal with these issues, we are not dealing with dollar bills and nickels and dimes and quarters. We are dealing with the very essence of who we are as people, what our priorities are, and what we really care most about. Our money is simply the life that we live, translated into the coinage of the day.

One problem we face when we talk about money is that sometimes we begin our discussion with some faulty assumptions— so in this lesson we have chosen the richest man who ever lived to be our consultant. His name is Solomon. What was Solomon's advice about money?

Solomon was responsible for the book of Ecclesiastes and the book of Proverbs. Scattered throughout these two books (and in some other passages in the Old Testament) are some profound thoughts about money.

If Solomon were here today, he would tell us to get rid of some of the assumptions that we may have formulated along the way. For example, when we ask people what they're trying to accomplish by working their heads off for more money, most will say one of three things: "I'm trying to find satisfaction," "I'm trying to achieve significance," or, "I'd like to have security." Solomon would step to the podium and say something about each of those subjects.

Before we hear from Solomon, however, let's look at some passages of Scripture in order to qualify Solomon as a consultant. Is he really somebody we can trust to talk to us about money?

First Kings 10:14 says that when Solomon was in control "The weight of gold that came to Solomon yearly was six hundred and sixty-six talents of gold." This hoard of money (approximately 25 tons!) was the tribute he exacted from the heathen nations around him. Twenty-five tons of gold! That's hard to comprehend.

First Kings 10:21 talks about Solomon's house: "All King Solomon's drinking vessels were gold, and all the vessels of the House of the Forest of Lebanon were pure gold. Not one was silver, for this was accounted as nothing in the days of Solomon." In Ecclesiastes 2:4–9 Solomon says:

> I made my works great, I built myself houses, and planted myself vineyards. I made myself gardens and orchards, and I planted all kinds of fruit trees in them. I made myself water pools from which to water the growing trees of the grove. I acquired male and female servants, and had servants born in my house. Yes, I had greater possessions of herds and flocks than all who were in Jerusalem before me. I also gathered for myself silver and gold and the special treasures of kings and of the provinces. I acquired male and female singers, the delights of the sons of men, and musical instruments of all kinds. So I became great and excelled more than all who were before me in Jerusalem. Also my wisdom remained with me.

Solomon was the greatest man who had lived up to that point, and he had more money than anyone had ever had. If there was one thing Solomon knew, it was money. He studied it, and he wrote in his journal—the book of Ecclesiastes—some of the thoughts he had about the three key issues mentioned above: satisfaction, significance, and security.

RISKY ASSUMPTIONS
Money Brings Satisfaction
Did Solomon find satisfaction in his money?

He writes in Ecclesiastes 5:10, "He who loves silver will not be satisfied with silver; nor he who loves abundance with increase. This also is vanity."

Do you know the problem in trying to find satisfaction in money? One little popular phrase really sums it up: "Everybody's yearning power is greater than their earning power." In other words, no matter how much you have, you never have "enough."

In fact, Ecclesiastes 4:8 says, "There is one alone, without companion: He has neither son nor brother. Yet there is no end to all his labors, nor is his eye satisfied with riches. But he never asks, 'For whom do I toil and deprive myself of good?' This also is vanity and a grave misfortune."

Solomon is saying that finding satisfaction in money is like grasping for the wind. You can never achieve it. You will never be satisfied because the never-ending problem is "How much is enough?" Most people never arrive at the place where they can say, "That's it. Now I have enough. Now I am satisfied."

Money Brings Significance

Some people feel that if they can get enough money, then they will have enough self-esteem, and everybody will respect them. What does Solomon say in Ecclesiastes 2:11? "Then I looked on all the works that my hands had done, and on the labor in which I had toiled; and indeed all was vanity and grasping for the wind. There was no profit under the sun."

Solomon said, "I tried to find significance in my quest for wealth, and I didn't find it." He was extremely wealthy, but he didn't find significance there.

Money Brings Security

Can we find security in money? Solomon penned some verses about security in money. Notice Proverbs 23:5: "Will you set your eyes on that which is not? For riches certainly make themselves wings; they fly away like an eagle toward heaven."

Ecclesiastes 5:11 says this: "When goods increase, they increase who eat them; so what profit have the owners except to see them with their eyes?" Solomon said that when we get more, that just multiplies the number of people who have to be supported by it. Some people have so much money they have to hire accountants, attorneys, consultants, people to take care of their stocks, and their payroll alone is more money than you and I will make in a lifetime. The more they make, the more they have to spend. And Solomon asks, "Where is the satisfaction and security in that?"

Ecclesiastes 6:2 offers another thought: "A man to whom God has given riches and wealth and honor, so that he lacks nothing for himself of all he desires; yet God does not give him power to eat of it, but a foreigner consumes it. This is vanity, and it is an evil affliction." Solomon is saying that we can make all kinds of money, but all of a sudden we look up and somebody else has it. Then what happens to our security?

Ecclesiastes 5:13–15 adds:

There is a severe evil which I have seen under the sun: riches kept for their owner to his hurt. But those riches perish through misfortune; when he begets a son, there is nothing in his hand. As he came from his mother's womb, naked shall he return, to go as he came, and he shall take nothing from his labor which he may carry away in his hand.

Why can't we find security in money? Because we can't take it with us.

We have nothing to our name when we're born, and there are no pockets in a burial shroud. What we do with what God gives us while we are on this earth makes the difference. We will never find security in money.

Some people think, "If I can just get a better portfolio. If I can just get a better investment plan. If I can just make sure that I can get all this stuff converted to precious metal. If I can just get it in a security deposit box." But in the final analysis, you could put it in the wrong place and lose it all, and then where will you be?

You are not going to find security in riches.

RIGHT ATTITUDES

Let's move from those risky assumptions and talk about some attitudes than can make a difference. What are some right attitudes toward money? Here are two that are very important.

Money Is a Gift From God

Ecclesiastes 5:19 tells us, "As for every man to whom God has given riches and wealth, and given him power to eat of it, to receive his heritage and rejoice in his labor—this is the gift of God." Whatever you have, it is a gift from God.

Deuteronomy 8:18 states it this way: "And you shall remember the Lord your God, for it is He who gives you power to get wealth, that He may establish His covenant which He swore to your fathers, as it is this day."

Money is a gift from God, and whatever we have, it's a gift from Him. We may think we have the energy to earn it, but where did that come from? God is behind it all, and we should give Him thanks for that.

Money Is to Be Enjoyed

Solomon says that money is to be enjoyed as a gift from God, which may surprise a lot of us. Many Christians think that once they get right on stewardship, they can't enjoy what God has provided for them. But in Ecclesiastes 7:14 Solomon wrote, "In the day of prosperity be joyful." However, he was careful to add, "But in the day of adversity consider. Surely God has appointed the one as well as the other, so that man can find out nothing that will come after him."

Solomon is saying we should learn how to be joyful when we have money, and also how not to be destroyed when we don't have very much. If God has blessed you and you are doing what is right as a generous, godly person, you don't have to apologize that you have some nice things. You don't have to be proud and arrogant about it—but you can enjoy them.

Do you ever thank God for your house? Do you ever stop and thank Him for those simple little things? Thank You, Lord, for a warm house. Thank you for a car that starts. Thank You for clothes that fit.

Of course, if God has blessed you, remember what Paul wrote in 1 Timothy 6:17: "Command those who are rich in this present age not to be haughty, nor to trust in uncertain riches but in the living God, who gives us richly all things to enjoy."

And listen to Ecclesiastes 6:9: "Better is the sight of the eyes than the wandering of desire. This also is vanity and grasping for the wind." What did Solomon mean? Most people are so busy getting more, they can't enjoy what they already have. You don't have to be rich to enjoy what you have; you just have to be able to enjoy what you have. We must learn how to be grateful and glad, not gloomy and greedy. And we all have so much to be thankful for. We operate as believers out of a heart of gratitude.

I believe the only people who have been able to put together this very delicate balance about life are the people of God who have come to grips with two facts: (1) that God has given them everything, and (2) that they are responsible to be stewards of that, and to return to God a specific portion of that which He has entrusted to them.

How do we keep the clutches of materialism from around our necks? By tithing. Every week that you sit down and deal with a paycheck that belongs to God, it causes many things to happen in your heart. Solomon put it this way in Proverbs 3:9–10. He said, "Honor the Lord with your possessions, and with the firstfruits of all your increase; so your barns will be filled with plenty, and your vats will overflow with new wine." The plan of action is to tithe.

Righteous Actions

There was a period of time in Israel's history when God's people forgot that the way to deal with materialism is by tithing. The people of Israel strayed from following God. All of a sudden, the wheels started coming off. They began to have problems. The culture began deteriorating.

So God called the prophet Malachi to instruct the people. Malachi preached a sermon to them, and he recorded it for us in a book with his name on it. And in the third chapter of Malachi, he talks about some righteous actions that we are to apply with money.

He tells us to take a tenth of everything God gives us and give it back to Him. He chides the people of Israel who have stopped tithing and blames their problems on that neglect.

The principles in the book of Malachi—returning to God the first ten percent of everything He gives us—will help us maintain equilibrium in our lives.

Tithing Is God's Way of Perpetuating His Program

We read in Malachi 3:10, "Bring all the tithes into the storehouse, that there may be food in My house." The phrase "food in My house" is an Old Testament euphemism meaning that the needs of the Levites and the priests would be met. God's plan is for God's people to take that which God has entrusted to them and to support the work they believe in.

Tithing Is God's Way of Pointing Out Our Priorities

In Malachi 1:8, the prophet addresses some of the people who were bringing inferior animal sacrifices to the Lord. He says, "'And when you offer the blind as a sacrifice, is it not evil? And when you offer the lame and the sick, is it not evil? Offer it then to your governor! Would he be pleased with you? Would he accept you favorably?' says the Lord of hosts."

He is saying, "When you tithe, give the best. Give it first. Don't give God the leftovers of your life." When we give God the best, it says something about our priorities and how important we think God's work is.

Tithing Is God's Way of Proving God's Promises

Malachi 3:10 again says, "Try Me now in this . . . if I will not open for you the windows of heaven and pour out for you such blessing that there will not be room enough to receive it." Do we believe that? Do we believe God can do that? God keeps His promises, and He doesn't lie. Tithing is God's way of proving His promises.

Tithing Is God's Way of Promoting Our Faith

Sometimes people come to me and say, "This doesn't make any sense. I looked at the bottom line as I added everything up, and I've got more going out than coming in already. This doesn't make any sense. But if God says it, I believe it; and I'm going to do it." But once they take the step and tithe, little by little God begins to make things change and happen. A lot of times He changes our attitudes, or He changes the things we think we have to have. Suddenly we discover that when we put God first and we operate out of the principle of faith, God builds our faith, and we grow from faith to faith.

Tithing Is a Way of Providing for Our Needs

Ninety percent goes farther when God is up front, for somehow God can take the 90 percent and make it worth more in the everyday economy of your life than a hundred percent would ever be if you put Him at the bottom. Put Him at the top. Take the first ten percent and give it to God, and watch what He does with the 90 percent that is left.

The more God gives you, the more He enables you to give back. It is a wonderful thing to watch God do this, and then to see Him provide for all of your needs.

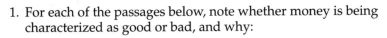

APPLICATION

1. For each of the passages below, note whether money is being characterized as good or bad, and why:

   Ruth 4:11

   1 Kings 3:7–13

   Esther 5:11

   Psalm 39:6

   Proverbs 13:7

Proverbs 14:24

Luke 16:13

2. What do you think the diversity of information about money in the above passages reveals?

   a. What basic principles seem to be common throughout?

3. Read Psalm 49:5–9 and Psalm 112:1–3.

   a. What is common to both of these people?

b. What is different about their positions in life?

c. What do you think makes them different in this way?

d. What would you guess is the top priority of the first?

e. Of the second?

f. What difference do you think that makes?

4. What was Paul's apparent attitude toward material possessions as reflected in Philippians 4:11–13?

   a. Why, if he was obedient to God, did Paul not have the riches spoken of in Psalm 112:1–3?

   b. What clue might Matthew 6:19–20 supply?

5. What insights into tithing do the passages below provide?

Leviticus 27:30

Numbers 18:21

Deuteronomy 14:22–23

2 Chronicles 31:2–5

Nehemiah 13:11–12

6. What motivation might we find in James 1:17 for Christian giving?

a. In your opinion, how should this affect each Christian?

DID YOU KNOW?

The same wealth that built Solomon's empire may well have destroyed it. How? The political alliances so vital to his economy led to his many political marriages, which in turn led to his many idolatrous wives, turning his heart away from God and His Word. The heavy taxation he levied on God's people led to the political intrigue and divisiveness that split God's nation immediately following Solomon's death. And the opulence and excesses of the royal court not only turned the hearts of the people away from Solomon, but turned many of their hearts cold toward God.

The lesson? Wealth in the hands of God, entrusted to a selfless steward, can accomplish much; but when the steward takes control, it can only lead to ruin.

TWO PORTFOLIOS

Selected Scriptures

In this lesson we examine the huge difference between the "portfolios" of investing in earthly treasure and investing in treasure in heaven.

OUTLINE

All of us, as we begin to serve the Lord, are involved in the investment process; and the Bible tells us there are two portfolios we are concerned about. Jesus, in fact, talked about these in Matthew 6:19–24.

I. **Portfolio One: Treasures on Earth**
   A. They Deteriorate and Depreciate
   B. They Demand Constant Vigilance and Care
   C. They Can Desensitize Us to the Needs of Others
   D. They Don't Go With You to Heaven
   E. They Can Drive You to Do Things You Don't Want to Do
   F. They Don't Satisfy Us Even Now
   G. They Are Doomed to Ultimate Destruction

II. **Portfolio Two: Treasures in Heaven**
   A. They Constantly Appreciate
   B. They Are Cared For by Someone Else
   C. They Continue for Eternity
   D. They Cause God to Be Pleased
   E. They Create Joy in the Body of Christ
   F. They Certify Your Passion in Life

III. **Two Principles of Investment**
   A. The Principle of Desire
   B. The Principle of Direction

In the simplest terms, Jesus said that the two ways we invest are in earthly treasures and in heavenly treasures. So let's see what happens when we invest in these two portfolios.

PORTFOLIO ONE: TREASURES ON EARTH

At the outset, let's not adopt the mistaken idea that what we do with our money here on earth is not important. God cares about what we do with money. In fact, many times in the New Testament He gives us instruction about what we are supposed to do. In 2 Corinthians 12:14, for example, He says, "The children ought not to lay up for the parents, but the parents for the children." So one thing we should be doing with our resources is to provide for our children.

The Bible also says in 1 Timothy 5:8 (KJV) that if anyone doesn't provide for his family, he is worse than an infidel. God expects us to care for our families and to provide for them.

And, in Luke 8:3, we are told that during the early part of Jesus' ministry, there were some women who "provided for Him from their substance." There were certain women who obviously had some resources, and they took out of those resources and made it possible for Jesus to carry on His work.

Having resources is not wrong—but it is wrong when resources have you. God tells us to be careful how we make investments in our earthly portfolio. He wants us to keep them in perspective, and the Bible tells us about investing in our earthly portfolio.

They Deteriorate and Depreciate

Matthew 6 tells us that earthly treasures are subject to ruin when the moths get them, subject to rust when they corrode, and subject to robbers who break in and steal.

When you put all your money into earthly things, you discover that they have a tendency to depreciate. Is the car you bought three years ago worth the same today as when you bought it? Though it may seem there are exceptions, earthly things don't normally appreciate.

They Demand Constant Vigilance and Care

Have you ever noticed that? In Matthew 6, thieves break in and steal. That's as common today as it was then. Burglars case a house, wait until the owners are gone, then break in and steal. Earthly treasures always have to be watched. We get a new toy or a new possession, and all of a sudden we are in the maintenance business. Whatever you invest in on the earth demands vigilance and care.

They Can Desensitize Us to the Needs of Others

You would think that the people who have the most are the people who do the most for God. But that's rarely true. Throughout the history of God's people, it hasn't been the people who have had the most who have given the most. It has usually been those who have the least, just as it was with the Macedonians in 2 Corinthians 8 who gave out of their poverty.

Sometimes, when we get a lot of stuff, we can become insensitive to the needs of hurting people if we are not careful.

There is a story in Luke 16 that illustrates this principle very well. A beggar was lying at the gate of a rich man, hoping to get a few crumbs from the rich man's table. And yet every time the rich man left his residence with the poor man lying there, nothing happened. He lived so far above the poverty of this man that he never even saw the connection. He was desensitized to the poor man's need.

Many wealthy Christians are extremely generous and sensitive, always looking for someone to help. Yet if someone invests exclusively in their earthly portfolio, they need to guard against the possibility of becoming insensitive to the needs of others.

They Don't Go With You to Heaven

First Timothy 6:7 tells us very clearly, "For we brought nothing into this world, and it is certain we can carry nothing out." You don't take it with you. You can send it ahead, but you can't take it with you. When you invest in your earthly portfolio, it is for the here and now—but it doesn't go past the grave.

They Can Drive You to Do Things You Don't Want to Do

There are many people with many things who would just like to go back to the simple life—but they can't. They're stuck. And they can actually end up doing a lot of stuff they don't want to do. In fact, 1 Timothy 6:9–10 says some interesting things about the problems that occur with a portfolio that is full, but full of earthly treasure only. It says,

> But those who desire to be rich fall into temptation and a snare, and into many foolish and harmful lusts which drown men in destruction and perdition. For the love of money is a root of all kinds of evil, for which some have strayed from the faith in their greediness, and pierced themselves through with many sorrows.

You can go through your life with so much in the resource fund that you get caught up in it and get off track. That's why in Luke 18:25 we read, "For it is easier for a camel to go through the eye of a needle than for a rich man to enter the kingdom of God." The Lord is saying that we have to be careful when we have lots of resources because if we are not careful, they can give us a false sense of security and make us think we have something we don't have; and then we are led astray.

They Don't Satisfy Us Even Now

You say, "Wait a minute." Have you ever heard people say, "If I just had more of this, and more of that, then I'd be happy"? But you know what? You are never happy! How much money is enough? I'll tell you how much is enough. Just a little bit more. The wisest and richest man on earth, King Solomon, concluded that "all was vanity and grasping for the wind. There was no profit under the sun" (Ecclesiastes 2:11).

They Are Doomed to Ultimate Destruction

All things material are going to burn up someday. Second Peter 3:10 tells us that the whole world is going to be burned up with everything in it. As we have said before, the only two things that survive are the eternal souls of men and the eternal Word of God.

Somebody once told me that if you want to keep a good perspective on all your earthly possessions, get a red tag and write on it "soon to be burned," and then tie the tag on whatever it is you've got. Then every time you look at that earthly possession, the tag will help you remember, "Well, this is nice for now, but it's not going to be here forever. It's all going up in smoke."

PORTFOLIO TWO: TREASURES IN HEAVEN

Let's examine five things about our heavenly portfolio that will encourage us as we begin to give to God.

They Constantly Appreciate

In Mark 10:29–30 we read,

> So Jesus answered and said, "Assuredly, I say to you, there is no one who has left house or brothers or sisters or father or mother or wife or children or lands, for My sake and the gospel's, who shall not receive a hundred fold now in this time—houses and brothers and sisters and mothers and children and lands, with persecutions—and in the age to come, eternal life."

Jesus said when you invest in eternal things, it just keeps appreciating out into eternity; you can never give to Him and not receive a hundredfold—that's a lot.

In fact, Luke 6:38 says when we give, God gives back—but He has a much better way of giving. Notice this: "Give, and it will be given to you: good measure, pressed down, shaken together, and running over will be put into your bosom." Jesus was talking about the giving that was involved in the gift of grain. He said that when you give to God, God loves to maximize your investment. When you put investments in your heavenly portfolio, they are always appreciating.

They Are Cared For by Someone Else

You don't have to worry about heavenly investments! Whatever you've got up there, God is taking care of it. Matthew 6 tells us that whenever we put our investment in heaven, it is not subject to ruin, rust, and robbery. It can't be touched, because God is taking care of it.

They Continue for Eternity

The returns on heavenly investments do not stop. In fact, John 6:27 says it this way: "Do not labor for the food which perishes, but for the food which endures to everlasting life, which the Son of Man will give you, because God the Father has set His seal on Him." When you invest in eternity, you invest in eternity. Whatever you give to God will never, ever go away. You invest for the Word of God, and it lives and abides forever. You invest in someone's life who is a Christian, and their soul goes on into eternity. When you invest in evangelism, God uses that to bring many sons to Himself, and they go to heaven. We truly are investing in a heavenly portfolio.

They Cause God to Be Pleased

The Bible says exactly that in Philippians 4:18. Paul said, "Indeed I have all and abound. I am full, having received from Epaphroditus the things sent from you, a sweet-smelling aroma, an acceptable sacrifice, well pleasing to God." When we give to the eternal investment priorities of the Word of God, the Bible says God is pleased. Is pleasing God your goal?

They Create Joy in the Body of Christ

When you invest in your eternal portfolio, not only is God pleased, but the people around you are blessed. Paul said that when he received the offering that was directed to him as a part of a church's eternal investment, it was a matter of great joy to him (Philippians 4:15–18).

They Certify Your Passion in Life

Matthew 6:24 says that we can't serve two masters, and we have to decide which one we are going to serve. The verse doesn't say we can't have money; it says we can't serve it. We can have money if we don't serve it. But if we serve money, we are the servant, and money is in control. Matthew 6:24 says we have to decide where we are going to put our priorities and how we are going to look at life.

Matthew 6:21 tells us, "For where your treasure is, there your heart will be also." Did you know that? Your treasure is like an anchor that pulls your heart in after it. Why do you think God wants us to put our treasure in heaven? Does He need our treasure? No, but He wants our hearts, doesn't He? When we put our treasure in heaven, our heart follows it.

TWO PRINCIPLES OF INVESTMENT

There are two principles of investment we should remember when we are making our investments, whether in the heavenly portfolio or in the earthly portfolio.

The Principle of Desire

Where is your heart? Where do you want your heart to be? Put your treasure in spiritual things, and you will find you have more concern about spiritual things. If you don't have a heart for those things but want one, this is how you do it. You put your treasure there first.

The Principle of Direction

Through whichever lens you look, that is the direction you will go. You have a choice. Many people view spiritual matters through their earthly portfolio, and it usually comes out like this: "I am going to see how everything works out down here, and if I have anything left that I can do, then I am going to do some things for God. But I am going to take care of this first."

The other way to look at it is to reverse that process and seek first the kingdom of God and His righteousness, and look at everything you do through God's portfolio of eternal investment; then watch what happens. This is a different way of looking at things.

Take that step and believe what God says is true. He will not disappoint you. He will do for you what He has promised.

1. What is evident from the following passages about some of the things riches cannot guarantee?

   Psalm 62:10–11

   Proverbs 11:4

   Proverbs 11:16

   Proverbs 11:28

   Proverbs 23:5

   Proverbs 27:24

   Jeremiah 9:23–24

2. What light does 1 Corinthians 3:11–15 shed on the idea of making eternal investments?

   a. How does this relate to 2 Corinthians 5:9–10?

b. How might both of these passages relate to Christian stewardship?

3. Read Hebrews 11:24–27. How great were the treasures in Egypt that were available to Moses?

a. What do you think is the "reward" to which Moses looked? (see Romans 8:18.)

b. What in this life did he get in return for giving up Egypt's riches?

c. What lesson might we take from this concerning stewardship?

4. What can we learn from 1 John 3:17 and Ephesians 4:28 about one way to "send it ahead"?

5. How does Psalm 1:1–3 unite the two concepts of earthly goods and eternal investments?

DID YOU KNOW?

A simple ritual observed at the close of the Jewish Shabbat (Sabbath) beautifully illustrates the concept of the two realms in which we live, possess and invest. A candle is lit representing one's life in the week ahead: only it is not one candle, but two. It bears the appearance of one because the two are so tightly interwoven, and because it burns with one flame. And yet it is distinctly two candles—representing the secular (material) and sacred (heavenly) sides of life. The ritual is performed as a reminder that in the week ahead, although the life is lived as one light, the secular and sacred should be remembered as distinctly separate—much like the concepts of earthly investments vs. heavenly ones.

SOWING AND REAPING

Galatians 6:7–10

This lesson carefully examines a principle that pervades the Word of God as well as the Christian life: whatever we sow, that's what we will reap.

OUTLINE

From the farmer in the field, to the non-Christian making a decision about the Gospel, to the Christian considering the wisdom of obedience, there exists in God's Word an overriding principle that governs the sustaining of His work in the world. That principle inevitably returns to the sower a harvest based on what he has sown.

I. **The Principle of Personal Deception**
   A. Be Not Deceived
   B. God Is Not Mocked
   C. Whatever a Man Sows, That He Will Also Reap

II. **The Principle of Moral Corruption**

God has established some absolute principles in His universe that operate in every sphere of living—principles that cannot be violated whether they be in the moral, spiritual, or physical realm. The principles that operate in all of the areas of life are basic and few; simple yet profound. They are principles God has ordained, and therefore they cannot be violated without the violator suffering a penalty.

In our text today—Galatians 6:7–10—one of those principles is summarized for us in the seventh verse: "For whatever a man sows, that he will also reap." Whatever a man sows, that's what he will reap. This principle of order and consistency is written into all of life, no matter what sphere you may examine. This principle is true in the moral realm, the physical realm, and the spiritual realm. And there are examples everywhere we look.

For instance, in the physical realm, God promised Noah after the flood that as long as the earth remained, seed time and harvest, sowing and reaping would not cease (Genesis 8:22). So if a farmer wants to have a harvest, he has to sow seed in his field; otherwise there will be no harvest. The kind of harvest he expects is dependent on the kind of seed he sows, for what he sows is what he is going to reap. This principle is true and inviolate in several specific aspects.

If the farmer wants barley, he must sow barley seed. He won't get barley from sowing wheat seed. The harvest you reap is according to the nature of what you sow.

If the farmer wants a good crop, it is imperative that he sow good seed.

If the farmer wants a large harvest, he must sow many seeds. Paul, writing to the Corinthians in 2 Corinthians 9:6, reminded them, "He who sows sparingly will also reap sparingly, and he who sows bountifully will also reap bountifully." The kind of harvest you get in the realm of agriculture is dependent on the nature, the quality, and the quantity of seed that is sown. You will not get anything different than what has been sown into the ground.

The principle we can learn and apply to all areas of life is this: the sowers—not the reapers—decide what the harvest will be. It is not the one who comes to gather up the harvest; it is the one who puts the seed in the ground. The sowers determine the harvest.

Sometimes we hear the expression today that someone is "sowing their wild oats," usually as an excuse for profligate living. But let no one be fooled: a person who determines to sow wild oats will reap a wild harvest.

Job 4:8 tells us, "Those who plow iniquity and sow trouble reap the same." And Hosea the prophet, in speaking to his contemporaries on one occasion (Hosea 8:7), warned them that they sow the wind, and they are going to reap the whirlwind, which is an Old Testament idiom for judgment.

Whatever a man sows, that is what he is going to reap.

Paul uses that principle in Galatians 6 to teach a truth about the way a ministry is to be supported. In context, he is writing about how we give to the church and how we support God's work. This principle is couched in the context of stewardship and financial responsibility. Notice verse 6: "Let him who is taught the word share in all good things with him who teaches." Paul is talking about supporting the ministry, giving to the church or to the place where the Word of God is taught.

The word translated "share in all good things" is a Pauline expression used several times in his letters to refer to liberal, gracious, abundant giving. It is the word *koinoneo*, which has almost become a familiar word to us today even in English, though it is a transliteration out of the Greek language. *Koinoneo* means to share in partnership, to fellowship together, to have something in common. A person who is involved in sharing is called someone who is involved in koinonia.

The apostle Paul is telling the church in Galatia that those who belong to the church and are blessed by the Word of God are to share what they have with those who teach the Word of God or with the ministry of the church. As the Word of God is sown into the hearts of the people, they are to sow back into the life of the church that which they are reaping spiritually and financially.

Paul is teaching us that in the realm of finances within the church, there is a principle at work. It cannot be violated. That principle is that whatsoever a man sows, that's what he is going to reap. The principle of sowing and reaping is continually at work within the ministry of Jesus Christ.

Also in this text are two principles we need to examine.

THE PRINCIPLE OF PERSONAL DECEPTION

The principle of sowing and reaping is an immutable principle of God; and in order to emphasize this, Paul prefaces the principle with both a command, "do not be deceived" and a statement, "God is not mocked." Let's look at those two things for a moment.

Be Not Deceived

The possibility of being deceived is presented often in the New Testament. The Lord Jesus speaks of Satan as a liar and as a deceiver. In 2 John 7 we are told that "many deceivers have gone out into the world."

In Ephesians 5:6 Paul admonishes in his letter to the Ephesian church, "Let no one deceive you with empty words."

In Galatians 3, He warns that church against the potential of deception. Paul tells us it is possible in the spiritual realm to be self-deceived, to rationalize in one's own mind. And he warns in Galatians 6 that the principle of sowing and reaping is not going to be violated—and if you are not careful, you will deceive yourself.

God Is Not Mocked

The word for "mocked" in the New Testament language is a strange sounding word (*mukterizo*), and comes from the root word for "nose." The essence of the phrase is, "Be not deceived. You cannot turn your nose up at God." In essence Paul is saying, "Don't sneer at God." The word actually came to be used in later language as an attempt to fool, outwit, or deceive someone. So over the course of Galatians Paul is saying, "Be careful that you don't deceive yourselves, but remember: God will not be deceived." It is possible to deceive yourself, but God will not be deceived.

Whatever a Man Sows, That He Will Also Reap

In the sowing and reaping areas of stewardship, there is perhaps more self-deception that goes on than in any other area of the ministry. Statistics tell us that 20 percent of the people in the church give 80 percent of the money, and about 15 to 20 percent of the people do not tithe or give anything close to what might be considered even a minimum standard for stewardship. These statistics indicate that the vast majority of church members in this country are involved in some form of self-deception. They've come to believe that even in light of all God says about not violating the principle of sowing and reaping, somehow they can. But God is not going to be fooled. He won't be mocked.

How do we deceive ourselves about sowing and reaping? First, we deceive ourselves when we say, "I can't afford to give. I have to wait until my house is in order, until I get better fixed financially, until things are going better, I've got more bills paid, I've got more income. Then I will begin to give to God as I know I should." Sounds good, doesn't it? In most areas of life, we don't buy things until we have the money. But the problem is this: The harvest out of which you intend to give is totally dependent on whether or not you are going to sow any seed now so the harvest can be harvested. It is a cycle. We can't get the harvest out of that which we hope to give until we sow some seed. Yet we will sit there thinking, "I won't sow any seed until I get the harvest." Thus we end up in a stalemate with God and with ourselves.

So how do we change that?

We have to break into the cycle wherever we are and begin to sow. No one ever began to give because they felt like they could afford it. They began to give because it is a command from God. We have to start with the sowing. No farmer ever starts with harvesting.

Another way that we become involved in self-deception is by rationalizing that we give our time to God, and therefore, we are not so responsible to give of our income. Now, it's good that we give our time to God because all of us should be involved in doing that. But nowhere in the Word of God do we find that it is possible to exchange the time we give to God for the responsibility for what we do with our funds.

A third way we rationalize is by telling ourselves, "I give to a broad spectrum of ministries, so I don't have to give so much to the church." Of course, I give to other ministries besides my church. I believe in ministries, and I give to ministries, and I think Christians should. But the focus of the New Testament is on the New Testament local church.

In 1 Corinthians 9:11, Paul used the principle of sowing and reaping as it relates to his giving of the Gospel to the church. He said, "If we have sown spiritual things for you, is it a great thing if we reap your material things?" Paul says that he sowed and the congregation reaped. In Galatians the Bible teaches that the congregation sows and the ministry reaps. The sowing and the reaping work both ways because the church is set up for the sowing and reaping principle to function. There is no other organization on the face of the earth like that.

Note, too, that the Bible prioritizes our giving on the basis of where we receive the Word of God. "Let him who is taught the word share in all good things with him who teaches" (Galatians 6:6).

This doesn't mean we shouldn't give to other organizations. We should. But we also need to remember that the New Testament church, the local church, is the vehicle of God's blessing in this generation.

The New Testament clearly focuses in on the household of faith. Notice Galatians 6:10: "Therefore, as we have opportunity, let us do good to all, especially to those who are of the household of faith." In other words, as you have opportunity, do good to all men. Have a wide spectrum in your giving—but don't forget to specifically prioritize the household of God because that is where the blessing of the Word of God comes to your life.

THE PRINCIPLE OF MORAL CORRUPTION

Notice that Galatians 6:8 tells us, "For he who sows to his flesh will of the flesh reap corruption." Does that mean it is wrong to sow to the flesh? Absolutely not. Every time you eat a meal, you are sowing to the flesh. Every time you buy a house, you are sowing to the flesh. Every time you go to the doctor, you are sowing to the flesh. Everyone has to sow to the flesh. If we don't sow to the flesh, the flesh dies.

But the Scripture also teaches that whatever you sow to the flesh is going to come back in corruption, or decay and death.

Everything you sow to the flesh is going to die. Money can buy food, but it can't buy appetite. Money can buy a bed, but it can't buy sleep. Money can buy a house, but it can't buy a home. Money can buy pleasure, but it can't buy happiness. Money we invest in the flesh can buy only those things which will ultimately corrupt.

In today's world, we can watch people as they take the time, energy, ability, and creativity God has entrusted to them, use those things to earn income, and then take every dime they have and sow it all back into the flesh. Yet the Bible simply says this: you are going to have a harvest one of these days, and your harvest is going to be based on what you have sown. If everything you have sown has been in the area of the flesh—your own life, your own appetites, your own wants, your own desires—and you have sown nothing to the Spirit, in the end all you are going to get is a sense of emptiness and despair. All the life will be taken out of you.

So how do we avoid that? Notice the next part of the verse: "but he who sows to the Spirit will of the Spirit reap everlasting life." The Bible says that everything we do by way of sowing to the Spirit is going to outlive us. It is going to be with us eternally. What we put in is what we get out. If we don't put anything into our spiritual life, we aren't going to get anything out of it.

The same is true in the financial realm. If we are not investing financially in the things of God, we are not going to reap of the things of God: the sense of blessing and priority and excitement He wants us to have. We cannot violate this principle. Whatever we sow, that's what we are going to reap.

We can rationalize it. We can deceive ourselves. But we can't mock God.

APPLICATION

1. What can we learn about sowing and reaping from the following passages?

    Proverbs 22:8–9

    Hosea 8:7

    2 Corinthians 9:6

2. Read Luke 9:57–62 and answer the following:

    a. What was the expressed intent of the speaker in verse 57?

    b. Why do you think Jesus replied the way He did in verse 58?

c. What may have been behind the excuse offered in verse 59?

d. Why did Jesus say what He said in verse 60?

e. Summarize the dialogue in verses 61–62.

f. What picture does Jesus offer in verse 62?

g. How might this passage illustrate the principle of priority—that is, which comes first (sowing or reaping)?

3. List at least five specific ways in which we "sow to the flesh" with our money on a daily or weekly basis.

a. How does each of these result in "corruption" or decay?

b. Does that make them bad investments?

c. What does that make them?

4. How does the broad context of 2 Corinthians 9:5–7 help us to better understand this principle?

a. What is the object of the giving?

b. To whom does it minister?

5. In light of Romans 6:23, at what point might we begin to understand this principle of sowing and reaping?

a. What effect should that have in our lives over time?

6. How might the perspective gained from the following verses help us to sow to spiritual things?

Romans 12:1–2

Colossians 3:1–3

Hebrews 12:1–2

DID YOU KNOW?

In our urban and suburban society, we tend to miss one great point about the agricultural illustrations the Word of God offers in relation to the "sowing and reaping" of our material assets. In our minds, we may picture a farm in Kansas or Nebraska with tractors and combines humming. At the end of the season, workers get compensated, bankers get their payments, and the owners bank whatever profits are left over.

But in the ancient Middle East, sowing and reaping represented a huge portion of every year's activities for the entire family. The weather, prospects for invasion by locusts or marauding thieves, and even ill health in the family could threaten a season's yield. Most important, if there were no harvest, there were no other options. In other words, that yield itself must come in order for there to be a future. The "reaping" after the "sowing"—which God had commanded be given first to Him—was the key to every family's very survival.

GRACE GIVING

2 Corinthians 8–9

In this lesson, we examine the attributes of true, biblical, godly grace giving.

OUTLINE

Like God himself, the type of giving that is reflective of God possesses certain attributes. And while knowledge of those attributes, or characteristics, cannot guarantee that we will be obedient in grace giving, understanding them should certainly motivate us to be a part of the kind of giving that has its source in the grace of God.

    I.   **Grace Giving Is Sacrificial**

   II.   **Grace Giving Is Spontaneous**

  III.   **Grace Giving Is Selfless**

  IV.   **Grace Giving Is Systematic**

   V.   **Grace Giving Is Spiritual**

  VI.   **Grace Giving Is Sincere**

 VII.   **Grace Giving Is Sharing**

VIII.   **Grace Giving Is Sufficient**

The highest level of stewardship that man can know is the stewardship of God's grace. Stewardship is not merely a percentage, but a matter of a Christian's total responsibility before God. When we come to grips with the grace of God that has been dispensed to all of us, we have the opportunity of living the way God wants us to live in the beautiful house called grace. The exciting and challenging principles of grace giving come from the New Testament.

GRACE GIVING IS SACRIFICIAL

In 2 Corinthians 8:1–3 we read, "Moreover, brethren, we make known to you the grace of God bestowed on the churches of Macedonia: that in a great trial of affliction the abundance of their joy and their deep poverty abounded in the riches of their liberality. For I bear witness that according to their ability, yes, and beyond their ability, they were freely willing."

Please notice some words in those verses that seem like they don't belong together: "great trial of affliction," "deep poverty," and "liberality." Those words don't fit with each other. Great trial of affliction and great poverty, coupled with liberality? In fact, the next verse says that these believers gave not only according to their ability, but beyond their ability. In other words, their giving was sacrificial and went past the ordinary. Their giving reached down beyond the normal limits. It was giving at the level of sacrifice.

You cannot study 2 Corinthians 8–9 without being persuaded that selfless giving, sacrificial giving, was very much a part of the early church. It was not a matter of the tithe. The tithe never enters the picture, though undoubtedly it was at least that much. The issue was purposeful, deliberate, sacrificial giving—consistent, cheerful, and thankful.

Grace giving is sacrificial giving. Sacrifice means giving up something you want in order to do something God wants you to do. And that is one of the high and lofty principles of grace giving.

GRACE GIVING IS SPONTANEOUS

Grace giving is not done out of a sense of obligation. There are many motives we can use for giving to God. Some people give to God because the general good of the church is at stake. Some feel group pressure. Some give out of pride or maybe the fear of embarrassment. Some give for pity's sake, or for social approval. Some Christians give for a tax advantage. However, the greatest motivation, the greatest desire, is to give to God willingly in order to be involved in His service.

Second Corinthians 8:3 states it this way: "For I bear witness that according to their ability, yes, and beyond their ability, they were freely willing." They desired to give. Second Corinthians 9:7 says it should not be "grudgingly or of necessity." Human nature causes us on occasion to give with a spirit of obligation; but grace giving is always done with a desire in one's heart to be involved.

The Macedonians not only gave willingly, they earnestly begged for the privilege to do so. They were excited about being involved. This principle elevates New Testament giving more than any other principle in the Old Testament. For in the New Testament it is not only the gift that is at stake, it is the giver. Their giving is not only the action, but the attitude of heart. It is not only the method of giving the gift, but it is the motivation behind it. And God teaches us that if we give out of a sense of duty without a willing spirit, we miss the whole purpose of grace giving which is to give willingly even as God has given willingly to us of His own Son.

By the way, grace giving is not only sacrificial and spontaneous, the Bible says that we are to give cheerfully. And while the word *hilaros* can be translated "cheerful," it is also the word from which we get "mercy seat" and "atonement." So when we give to God, we are involved in a very high, lofty, and theologically wonderful ministry of giving to a great God. And we do it willingly.

Grace Giving Is Selfless

Verse 4 says, "imploring us with much urgency that we would receive the gift and the fellowship of the ministering to the saints." Human nature usually finds its focus in its own needs, but grace giving always focuses on the needs of others. Grace giving always sees beyond self to the needs that are out there. When we give and try to hang on to what we give, we violate the New Testament.

Grace Giving Is Systematic

In 2 Corinthians 8:6 we read, "So we urged Titus, that as he had begun, so he would also complete this grace in you as well."

Form and structure for giving in that church is implied here. Paul commanded the Corinthians (and us) to complete this grace, implying a structure in which we might grow. He said that Titus had already started to teach this information and help them understand what is involved in being godly stewards.

Sometimes we get the idea that Christian giving is a spontaneous thing that never has any plan to it, or that we should never be involved in any purposeful giving. But that's not the picture presented by the New Testament. In fact, in this context they spent a whole year planning for the offering, making sure that it was organized and put together right. Then, when the offering was to be delivered, they made sure they had competent people to deliver it, and ensured that it was delivered as it should have been. There was a system involved.

GRACE GIVING IS SPIRITUAL

Sometimes we talk about stewardship as though it is a necessary evil we have to put up with so the church can pay its bills. But when we say that, we miss the whole point. Stewardship is a spiritual reality that is just as much a part of our spiritual lives as Bible reading, prayer, and witnessing. Notice how this is brought out in 8:7: "But as you abound in everything—in faith, in speech, in knowledge, in all diligence, and in your love for us—see that you abound in this grace also." Paul says you have faith, you believe in speaking and bold utterance, you believe in knowledge, you believe in diligently living the Christian life, and you believe in love because you have sent your love to us—now start abounding in the grace of stewardship because it is on the same level as all the rest of these things.

GRACE GIVING IS SINCERE

Notice in 8:8–9, "I speak not by commandment, but I am testing the sincerity of your love by the diligence of others. For you know the grace of our Lord Jesus Christ, that though He was rich, yet for your sakes He became poor, that you through His poverty might become rich."

Paul wants to teach us in these two passages that our giving is to be a sincere reflection of our love relationship with God. He says that grace provokes the believer to confirm the sincerity of his love by enhancing the work of God in a tangible way.

GRACE GIVING IS SHARING

Notice in verses 12–15 how Paul expresses this concept:

> For if there is first a willing mind, it is accepted according
> to what one has, and not according to what he does not
> have. For I do not mean that others should be eased
> and you burdened; but by an equality, that now at this
> time your abundance may supply their lack, that their
> abundance also may supply your lack—that there
> may be equality. As it is written, "He who gathered
> much had nothing left over, and he who gathered little
> had no lack."

Paul is saying that the purpose of stewardship, and especially
God's wonderful program of stewardship, is that the needs of
the body and the needs of the world might be met through an
equitable plan. Who could have thought of this but God himself?
If we had done it, we would have established a quota that would
have been the same for everybody; but God says the kind of
sharing involved in stewardship is a perfect plan so the needs of
the body might be met.

He that has much is able to share much. He that has a little is
able to share of his little. But as we share proportionately that which
God has entrusted to us, the needs of the whole body are met.

Paul teaches us that the critical issue is the attitude of heart,
not the amount of the offering. He does not say you have to get to a
certain level of financial stability before you get involved in giving.
He says it is not important how much you have, or how much you
don't have. What is important is what you do with that which God
has entrusted to you.

The decision is not easy, and there will be struggles along the
way. But every struggle we have is worthwhile if it gets us to
the place of honesty before God. Grace giving is a matter of sharing
that which God has given to us.

GRACE GIVING IS SUFFICIENT

Second Corinthians 9:8 says, "And God is able to make all
grace abound toward you, that you, always having all sufficiency
in all things, may have an abundance for every good work." This
verse is given as a promise to the men and women who understand
the rest of the context, which is found in verse 7: "So let each one

give as he purposes in his heart, not grudgingly or of necessity; for God loves a cheerful giver."

Second Corinthians 9:8, in essence, is a cycle:

God is able
That's the might of it.

To make all grace
That's the measure of it.

Abound
That's the manner of it.

Toward you
That's the motion of it.

That you, always having all sufficiency in all things
That's the means of it.

May have an abundance for every good work
That's the ministry of it.

Because God is able
That's the might of it.

That is God's cycle of sufficiency and it just keeps going around. God says that when we get involved with Him in ministry, and we get involved in every good work, including the work of stewardship, we get involved in a sufficiency cycle which can never run dry if God's Word is true.

Now He doesn't say we will have all we want. But He says He is able to make all grace abound so that we will always have all sufficiency needed for the ministry God has called us to within the body.

1. Read Deuteronomy 15:7–11. In this command concerning care for the poor in Israel, what seems to be of equal concern to God?

   a. How would you describe God's concern for actions as compared to attitudes?

2. In Proverbs 30:7–9, what seems to be of greatest concern to the believer?

   a. What risks does he recognize in poverty?

   b. In wealth?

   c. How might this influence our attitudes toward stewardship?

3. Read Jeremiah 9:23–24. How would you describe the relationship of material things to spiritual things, according to this passage?

   a. How might this attitude influence your giving?

4. What observations about grace giving can you draw from the following passages?

2 Samuel 24:21–23

1 Kings 17:8–16

John 6:5–11

Acts 5:1–11

5. Read 2 Corinthians 8:1–9:15. What outward circumstances are described in 8:1–4, and how did they affect giving?

a. What, according to 8:5, did the giving believers do first?

b. In 8:8–9, is the foundation for the grace giving practiced by believers?

c. In 9:1–2, what was the effect of selfless giving on other believers?

d. In 9:8–11, what are the "all" and "every" effects of godly grace giving?

e. What is the "gift" of verse 15?

f. Why do you think it is mentioned in this context, and in this way?

DID YOU KNOW?

The very concept of "grace" is grounded in the idea of a "gift." The New Testament word "charis," translated "grace" in over 190 New Testament occurrences, nearly always denotes that which is bestowed on another without consideration of merit or worthiness. Various New Testament Greek lexicons offer synonyms that include "favor," "care," "help," "goodwill," and "benevolence."

While all of these can clearly be seen as pictures of that grace which God has bestowed on us in salvation, we would do well to view them, too, as pictures of the grace giving God would have us, as Christians, practice. That, in fact, is precisely the connection the Bible makes between the grace we have received and the grace we are to extend to others.

HIDING IN ALL THE WRONG PLACES

2 Corinthians 8–9

In this lesson we examine why some believers do not engage in the discipline of Christian stewardship.

OUTLINE

When all is said and done, it is not merely because of ignorance that some believers do not participate in giving willingly, systematically, and gratefully to the church. Some Christians either keep a convenient distance between themselves and God's principles, or they assume that they somehow have been exempted from His commands as well as His principles. But is that really true?

Why do some not give, and what are the answers to their objections?

I. **People Do Not Give Because They Are Not Concerned With God's Work**

II. **People Do Not Give Because They Are Not Convinced That They Are Responsible**

III. **People Do Not Give Because They Cannot Commit Themselves to Do It**

IV. **People Do Not Give Because They Are Not Courageous Enough to Trust Him**

V. **People Do Not Give Because They Are Not Careful About Life's Priorities**

VI. **People Do Not Give Because They Are Not Christians**

The story is told of a pastor who phoned the home of some of his recent church visitors, and a voice answered "Hello?"

The pastor said, "Who is this?"

There was a little whisper on the other end. It said, "This is Jimmy."

The pastor said, "How old are you, Jimmy?"

He said, "I'm four."

"Jimmy, may I please speak to your mom?"

"She's busy."

"Then can I speak to your dad?"

"He's busy, too."

"Are there any other adults at your home?"

"The police."

"Well, could I speak to one of the police officers?"

"They're busy."

"Who else is there?"

"The firemen."

"Put one of the firemen on the phone."

"They're busy."

"Jimmy, what are they all busy doing?"

"They're looking for me."

Some Christians are just like Jimmy. They've been hiding. Hiding is a pastime that started in the Garden. The whole business of hiding began as early as the first chapters of the book of Genesis when Adam and Eve hid from God. But how in the world can you hide from God?

When it comes to the matter of their responsibility in stewardship, some people have a tendency to hide. They hide from God and His Word. They try to hide from principles they know are true.

As we saw in Lesson Four, the book of Malachi teaches five principles about tithing that are very clear.

1. Tithing is God's way of perpetuating His program.
2. Tithing is God's way of pointing out our priorities.
3. Tithing is God's way of proving His promises.
4. Tithing is God's way of promoting our faith.
5. Tithing is God's way of providing for our needs.

These principles from God's Word are familiar to us. But the question is, if these are so clear, and they have been taught so many times, why is it that some people still do not give to God?

PEOPLE DO NOT GIVE BECAUSE THEY ARE NOT CONCERNED WITH GOD'S WORK

Some folks are busy with every other thing, and it never dawns on them that they should have thoughts about the work of God. This pattern is easy to get into. Maybe you have grown up in that kind of environment at home. But until you get concerned about the work of God, you will have a hard time being excited about giving to His work.

Turning once again to 2 Corinthians 8, we see that Paul frequently mentions people having a concern for the work. For instance, in 8:4 he says, "imploring us with much urgency that we would receive the gift and the fellowship of the ministering to the saints." There was an urgency here about ministering to the saints because they cared about the saints.

In verse 9 we see the same point: "For you know the grace of our Lord Jesus Christ, that though He was rich, yet for your sakes He became poor, that you through His poverty might become rich." In other words, the whole focus of giving is not ourselves, but how God uses our giving to touch others. And again in verse 16 we read the same kind of thought: "But thanks be to God who puts the same earnest care for you into the heart of Titus."

Giving starts first with a command from God, but it is fueled in our hearts by the fire of compassion for the many people who need the Word of God. How many people in your community need

God? How many people in your family need the Word of God? Through the teaching of the Word of God in our churches, on the radio and television, and in written literature, they can hear. This is done when God's people, with their generous giving, make it possible for churches and classrooms to be built, ministries to go forward, and community outreach to take place.

The Bible says that if you have a willing mind to give to God, it doesn't matter how much you have; it matters whether you are willing to have a compassionate heart to reach out to others. "For if there is first a willing mind, it is accepted according to what one has, and not according to what he does not have" (2 Corinthians 8:12).

God saved us not just to take us to heaven. He saved us for a purpose while we are here on earth. Every day we ought to be looking up into His face and saying, "Almighty God, what do You want me to do today? What can I do to advance the cause of Christ today? How can I serve? How can I invest? How can I minister?" Someday we are all going to give an account, but we can only do what we do while we are here.

People Do Not Give Because They Are Not Convinced That They Are Responsible

Wherever people are serious about the Word of God, you will find them tithing or practicing some form of it because it is a principle straight from God's Word.

Notice 2 Corinthians 8:6–7: "So we urged Titus, that as he had begun, so he would also complete this grace in you as well. But as you abound in everything—in faith, in speech, in knowledge, in all diligence, and in your love for us—see that you abound in this grace also." Paul admonishes us to see that we do all these other good things; but he says to be sure you abound in the grace of giving, too. Giving is a responsibility before God.

Look at verses 10 and 11: "And in this I give advice: It is to your advantage not only to be doing what you began and were desiring to do a year ago; but now you also must complete the doing of it; that as there was a readiness to desire it, so there also may be a completion out of what you have." Paul is telling the Corinthian believers that it is not enough just to desire to do it. He is saying, "Just do it!" It is an important responsibility from God.

And look in 2 Corinthians 9:4–5:

"Lest if some Macedonians come with me and find you unprepared, we (not to mention you!) should be ashamed of this confident boasting. Therefore I thought it necessary to exhort the brethren to go to you ahead of time, and prepare your generous gift beforehand, which you had previously promised, that it may be ready as a matter of generosity and not as a grudging obligation."

Paul said, "I'm preaching this truth to you because it is an important truth."

One out of every six verses in Matthew, Mark, and Luke has to do with money. And someone has calculated that, if you take all of the words of Jesus that are recorded for us in the Bible, He said more about money than He said about heaven or hell. Why would He do that? Because of all of the tangible things you can touch, money better represents your identity, your life, your values, and what you believe in. Jesus knew that if He could get a man's heart right about money, his heart would be right about other things.

That's why, when Jesus met the rich young ruler, He told him to go and sell everything he had. Did Jesus want him to become a pauper? No. He knew where that man's heart was. He put His finger right on the problem in the man's heart. He said, "Go sell everything you have," and the Bible says that the man walked away sadly.

Money is God's way of helping us to see who we are. Money helps us to understand what we believe in. Money is the most powerful, tangible expression of life. Money is the way God helps us to see where our priorities are.

If a person is not convinced that he is responsible before God, then he has failed to read Scripture. But you can't believe something out of existence. It is the Word of almighty God himself—and you can obey it, or you can disobey it. But you cannot ignore it.

There is not one believer who hasn't struggled along this path until they finally said, "Okay, God. You said it. I believe it. That settles it. We're not going to argue about this any more. Let's just go on and get it done."

When you do that, God begins to bless your life.

People Do Not Give Because They Cannot Commit Themselves to Do It

For the first time in the history of America, people are more willing to give than they are willing to commit to give. In years past, we would receive a certain number of stated commitments to give, and then we would pray that they would all come in. Usually we could assume that about 80 percent of those commitments would be fulfilled.

Today, it is different. People would rather give to something than commit to it. So now when we get written commitments, the gifts exceed the commitments. Why? Because we're a generation that wants to keep our options open as long as we can. If I commit to something, then I have said I am going to do that no matter what.

But if I can hedge that commitment, or not commit at all, then in my heart I can say, "Well, I'm planning to do it, but if things get tight down the road, I'm going to leave the door open so that nobody knows what I really said in my heart." So we would rather give than commit.

Yet when we read the Scriptures, we discover that commitments are part of the process of giving. Review 2 Corinthians 8:3, and notice the word: "For I bear witness that according to their ability, yes, and beyond their ability, they were freely willing."

Verse 11 says it a different way: ". . . Now you also must complete the doing of it; that as there was a readiness to desire it, so there also may be a completion out of what you have."

Notice verse 12: "For if there is first a willing mind . . . ." There is the commitment in heart and mind.

Second Corinthians 9:2 says, "For I know your willingness"; 9:5 adds, "Therefore I thought it necessary to exhort the brethren to go to you ahead of time, and prepare your generous gift beforehand, which you had previously promised, that it may be ready as a matter of generosity and not as a matter of grudging obligation."

And 9:7 says, "God loves a cheerful giver." So the commitment comes out of our heart and our willingness.

Giving must be a matter of willing commitment.

People Do Not Give Because They Are Not Courageous Enough to Trust Him

Trusting God takes courage. We often joke about the fact that once we are saved we are willing to trust God for eternity, but we are not willing to trust Him for next week. Eternity is a long time. If we can trust God to take us to heaven, don't you think we can trust God to bless us if we give to Him?

Some people say, "Well, I can't start giving to God until I get out of this financial mess." No, you start giving to God. That's the best way to get out of the financial mess! If it's true that God blesses those who give to Him, what you're going to need to get out of the mess you're in is a good blessing. If you wait until you get all the way through, you will first forget how badly you needed God; and second, you probably won't ever get there to begin with. When you put God first, that's the best first step toward getting right financially and fiscally in every way.

Second Corinthians 9:6 reminds us, "But this I say: He who sows sparingly will also reap sparingly, and he who sows bountifully will also reap bountifully." Now notice verses 10–11: "Now may He who supplies seed to the sower, and bread for food, supply and multiply the seed you have sown and increase the fruits of your righteousness, while you are enriched in everything for all liberality, which causes thanksgiving through us to God."

And then notice this great promise in chapter 9:8: "And God is able to make all grace abound toward you, that you, always having all sufficiency in all things, may have an abundance for every good work."

Do we believe God was telling the truth when He said that? Notice: "[He] is able to make all grace abound toward you, that you always having all sufficiency in all things, may have abundance for every good work."

Proverbs 3:9–10 says, "Honor the Lord with your possessions, and with the firstfruits of all your increase; so your barns will be filled with plenty, and your vats will overflow with new wine." Yet some people don't give because they are not courageous enough to trust God. Be courageous one step at a time. Just say, "Okay, I'm going to do it. I'm going to trust You. God, You show me."

PEOPLE DO NOT GIVE BECAUSE THEY ARE NOT CAREFUL ABOUT LIFE'S PRIORITIES

A lot of folks want to do right, but they just don't take care of first things first. You may not have money to buy this or that, but you do it anyway; suddenly you realize you just went shopping on God's money.

In 2 Corinthians 8–9, we learn that we are supposed to begin and complete. Maybe you aren't organized. Some temperaments are organized; others are not. If you're not, then you just have to sit down and make a point of it. You need to decide before the fact, "This is what I am going to do."

You can't be careless about this. The Bible says the people who have given have determined beforehand and made a special point of it. This decision is not from emotion; rather, it has been a very logical decision in response to God's Word.

PEOPLE DO NOT GIVE BECAUSE THEY ARE NOT CHRISTIANS

I'm not saying that if you don't give to God you are not a Christian. I am saying that it is possible for you to go to church and not be a Christian. And after all, if you haven't given your heart to the Lord, why would you want to give Him anything else? The starting point in giving to God is to give Him your heart. Paul says the Macedonians first gave themselves. Second Corinthians 8:5 reads, "And not only as we had hoped, but they first gave themselves to the Lord, and then to us by the will of God." The first gift that you give to God is yourself!

If I weren't a Christian, if I didn't know Jesus Christ as my personal Savior, if I was not in love with Him, I would not want to give to the church. But I love Jesus Christ with all my heart. How can I help but love Him when I look at what He has done for me? And that's where it starts.

If you will give your heart to Christ, He will take care of all the rest. If your heart belongs to Him, He will give you a "want-to" where you don't have it right now. Far more important than anything else is this: the Lord Jesus Christ, who was rich, became poor for us that we who were poor might be made rich in Him.

If you will put your trust in Him, He will give you a clean heart, a new set of desires, new goals, and a new purpose in life.

If you have never given your life to Christ, you can do that right now by simply saying in your heart, "Lord, God, I know I am a sinner and I cannot save myself. I put my trust in You and You alone for eternal life. Now, Lord Jesus, come into my heart, forgive my sin, and give me eternal life."

If you will do that, the Lord Jesus will have your heart. That's where it all begins.

APPLICATION

1. Second Timothy 4:9–11 was written by Paul from prison when his execution seemed imminent. What do we find here about the fault of not being concerned about God's work? Who in this passage obviously was concerned? What do you think that may have cost him?

   a. Read 1 Corinthians 3:11–15, and consider: To whom does this appear to refer, Christians or non-Christians?

   b. To what time period does this seem to refer: during one's life or some point after death?

c. What is it that will be tested? Do you think that includes the work of Christian stewardship?

d. By what will they be tested? Do you think this is literal or figurative?

e. In light of 2 Corinthians 5:10, who will do the testing? With what result(s)?

f. How do you think these outcomes will compare with wealth and achievement in this world?

3. Read Ephesians 1:1–14 and answer the following:

a. What terms of abundance or plenty can you find in this passage?

b. What other terminology of benefits or blessing can you find?

c. How many of the good things described in this passage are the result of something the believer has done?

d. In light of this passage, how might a believer respond in a tangible way to all God has done?

4. What is likely to be the unbeliever's outlook on Christian stewardship, according to 1 Corinthians 2:14?

5. What does 2 Corinthians 5:17–20 indicate is the first priority for the unbeliever?

6. How has this lesson affected your own perspective on giving to God and His work?

DID YOU KNOW?

One of the factors in ancient Israel that created confused people like the "rich young ruler" was a popular belief based on a misunderstanding of God's Word. In Deuteronomy 28, God had made it very clear to Israel that if the nation obeyed Him, He would bless it; and if it disobeyed Him, He would bring harsh discipline. This simple principle was twisted by the religious leaders of Christ's day to mean, "If you are rich, God has blessed you for your righteousness; and if you are poor, God has cursed you for your unrighteousness."

What that meant for the religious leaders was that their wealth "justified" them before God—not to mention giving them ample excuse to ignore God's priorities, such as the poor within the household of faith. No wonder the rich young ruler went away distressed. He was unwilling to admit that instead of needing his own righteousness based on what he had, he needed God's righteousness based on Who He is!

FIVE PICTURES
OF GOD'S PROVISION

Selected Scriptures

This lesson ensures that any believer who wants to examine what the Scriptures say about God's provision for those who give to Him has the best pictures possible from His Word.

OUTLINE

As we near the end of our discussion of stewardship, we may know tithing is something we should do—but we may not be sure it is all going to work out.

Though some people may not be motivated by rewards, the Bible does speak of rewards, just as the Bible speaks of God's provision. In Matthew 19:29, Jesus said, "And everyone who has left houses or brothers or sisters or father or mother or wife or children or lands, for My name's sake, shall receive a hundredfold, and inherit eternal life." God rewards in a bountiful, wonderful way those who honor Him. And in the Bible we find some vivid pictures of that provision.

   I.   **God's Cycle of Sufficiency**

  II.   **The Windows of Heaven**

 III.   **The Bank in Heaven**

 IV.   **Full Barns and Overflowing Vats**

  V.   **God's Incredible Harvest Law**

God's Cycle of Sufficiency

Let's examine five key passages related to giving and provide ourselves with information about how good stewardship is to our benefit as believers.

First, let's consider 2 Corinthians 9:7–8: "So let each one give as he purposes in his heart, not grudgingly or of necessity; for God loves a cheerful giver. And God is able to make all grace abound toward you, that you, always having all sufficiency in all things, may have an abundance for every good work."

I would like to repeat the picture of God's wonderful cycle of sufficiency. Although we touched on this cycle briefly in Lesson Seven, it would be good for us to review it:

God is able
That's the might of it.

To make all grace
That's the measure of it.

Abound
That's the manner of it.

Toward you
That's the motion of it.

That you, always having all sufficiency in all things
That's the means of it.

May have an abundance for every good work
That's the ministry of it.

Because God is able
That's the might of it.

This brings us full circle, back to where we started. God gives to us all grace abundantly so we have all sufficiency in all things. The purpose is that we in turn can do every good work. And it begins all over again. As we continue to invest, as we continue to trust, God continues to provide.

As we give to Him, He enables us to have what we need so that we can give more. And the more we give, the more He provides, and the more He provides, the more we can serve Him.

The Bible teaches that as we trust God with our resources, He provides the sufficiency we need to continue to minister and to continue to serve. You can trust God. You can count on the fact that while you are on the threshold of this decision (and it is a frightening threshold), what pushes you over the edge is this truth: God can be trusted. He will provide.

God's cycle of sufficiency is one way we know that He can be trusted to provide.

THE WINDOWS OF HEAVEN

Now let's look at Malachi 3:10: "'Bring all the tithes into the storehouse, that there may be food in My house, and try Me now in this,' says the Lord of hosts, 'If I will not open for you the windows of heaven and pour out for you such blessing that there will not be room enough to receive it.'"

When I think of giving, and I begin to worry about whether or not I can give or trust God with it, I need to put in my mind this picture. God in heaven has shown that when I am faithful to Him, He will open up that gigantic window in heaven and pour out a blessing upon me that is so incredibly great I will not be able to receive it.

The Bible does not say that all the blessings will be financial—although they may be. But the people in the kingdom of God who are the most blessed are those who have taken this truth to heart, and now practice it day in and day out. God has promised in His Word to bless us and to fill our cup with blessing so that we will always have what we need. Malachi 3:10 is the picture of the open window.

THE BANK IN HEAVEN

The third passage is Philippians 4:19: "And my God shall supply all your need according to His riches in glory by Christ Jesus." If we go back and look at Philippians 4 in context, we see that it is a financial passage. People often quote this verse in reference to other things, as if the verse were theirs unconditionally. But it is not an unconditional promise. This verse is a conditional promise based on what God has talked about in the rest of the passage—which has to do with trusting Him as we give. God, through the apostle Paul, says to us, "You don't have to worry when you are faithful in your giving, for your God in heaven will supply all your need according to His riches in glory by Christ Jesus."

The picture I believe the Bible offers here is that God has a heavenly bank. When you give, you are making an investment, and the investment is for eternity. The investment is in the incredible bank of heaven, with Jesus Christ himself as the chief executive officer.

This passage says that God will supply our need from that resource. And notice, too, five characteristics of His promise:

1. His promise is personal: "my God."
2. His promise is positive: "shall supply."
3. His promise is pointed: "all of your need."
4. His promise is plentiful: "according to His riches in glory."
5. And His promise is powerful: It is in "Christ Jesus" himself.

We need to notice that it does not say, "My God shall supply all you need out of His riches in glory." If I am wealthy and I am asked to give to a certain cause, and I give *out of* what I have, it could be any amount, from small to great. But if I give *according* to what I have, then the measure is incredibly greater. God has not promised to supply to us *out of* His bank. He is saying, "Look at the assets in this bank. Look at what I have. I am going to supply for you *according* to what I have." And that means His provision is so much greater.

FULL BARNS AND OVERFLOWING VATS

The fourth reference is Proverbs 3:9–10: "Honor the Lord with your possessions, and with the firstfruits of all your increase; so your barns will be filled with plenty, and your vats will overflow with new wine."

In Old Testament times, barns and vats were the basis of the economy. So the picture is one of productiveness even to the point of excess. God doesn't want to provide for you only minimally. He doesn't want to give you just enough so you can get by. He wants to prove to you that if you trust Him, if you take Him at His word, He is a God of abundance. He wants to give you more than you can imagine.

The Lord of Glory has said, "I am going to do this. I am going to provide your needs." And He has many wonderful ways to do that.

At one point in the early history of Dallas Seminary, shortly after it was founded in 1924, it almost folded. The seminary came to the point of bankruptcy, and all of the creditors were ready to foreclose at twelve noon on a particular day. That morning the founders of the school met in the president's office to pray that God would provide. In the prayer meeting was a Bible teacher by the name of Harry Ironside, a great theologian and writer. When it was his turn to pray, he reportedly said in his refreshingly candid way, "Lord, we know that the cattle on a thousand hills are Thine. Please sell some of them and send us the money."

Just about noon, while the meeting was still going on, a tall Texan in boots and open-collar shirt strolled into the seminary's business office. "Howdy," he said to the secretary. "I just sold two carloads of cattle over in Fort Worth and I've been trying to make a business deal go through, but it just won't work, and I feel God wants me to give this money to the seminary. I don't know if you need it or not, but here's the check." And he handed it over to the secretary.

The secretary took the check and, knowing something of the critical nature of the hour that was upon them, she went to the door of the prayer meeting and timidly tapped on the door. Dr. Lewis Sperry Chafer, the founder and president of the school, answered the door, and took the check from her hand. The check was for the exact amount of their debt. Then he recognized the name of that cattleman on the check, and he knew it was a cattleman's check. Turning to Dr. Ironside he said, "Harry, God sold the cattle."

Can that really happen? Yes, not only on an institutional level, but on a personal level, too.

Before Donna and I left for Dallas Seminary as a young couple to study for the ministry, I went downtown to close out my checking account at the local bank in Cedarville. They were glad to see me because they said I was overdrawn by 80 dollars. I didn't think that was humanly possible because I was very careful; but they said, "No, we can't let you out of here." So I had to find 80 bucks just to close out my account.

Once we got to Dallas, we had enough money for two weeks. We figured we would get jobs and be in great shape. Well, we got jobs about halfway through the second week—but we would have to wait two weeks for our first paychecks. So about three weeks into our seminary journey, we didn't have a penny. We lived on macaroni and cheese dinners, which at the time cost 21 cents, until we couldn't even afford those. We had committed at the beginning of our marriage to make giving to God a priority; and just when we were at the very end of our rope, we received a letter from the bank in Cedarville. The letter said, "We just went through our monthly audit, and we have discovered that we deposited one of your deposits to your father's account. Here is a check for $210. Please forgive us for the inconvenience."

I thought, "It's not an inconvenience. God just sent it ahead and banked it for us until we needed it."

Everyone who has given to the Lord as a priority has a story like that in which God has miraculously provided in some unusual way, so that they would have what they needed. This is the principle of the full barns and the overflowing vats.

GOD'S INCREDIBLE HARVEST LAW

Let's close with one last promise—Luke 6:38. "Give, and it will be given to you: good measure, pressed down, shaken together, and running over will be put into your bosom. For with the same measure that you use, it will be measured back to you."

Galatians presents it this way: If you sow little, you will reap little. If you sow much, you will reap much. You reap what you sow. This is God's wonderful picture of the harvest law.

This may be the most powerful verse in Scripture concerning what happens to us when we give to the Lord. What does the harvest law say? Let's review:

- You reap only if you sow. If you don't sow, you don't reap.
- You reap only what you sow. If you sow corn, you don't reap beets.
- If you sow beets, you don't reap corn. Whatever you sow, the principle of identity says reap according to what you sow.
- You reap more than you sow. Put one seed into the ground, and the ratio of return is incredible.
- You reap later than you sow. The farmer does not reap his harvest on the day he puts seed into the ground. Sometimes we want a harvest the same day. We put the seed in the ground in the morning, and we go out at night wanting the plant to be full grown. We don't reap the day we sow; we reap later than we sow.

Some sow only a little bit and then ask, "Where's the harvest?" The harvest comes after the sowing, and we have to be willing to wait for the interval.

Hebrews 6:10 says, "For God is not unjust to forget your work and labor of love which you have shown toward His name, in that you have ministered to the saints, and do minister."

God's harvest law says that if you put seed into the ground, you will reap a harvest. God said it, and because God said it, you can believe it.

When we put together all of these pictures, we can understand one simple thing: We cannot use as an excuse for not giving to God the misconception that He will not provide because if we say that, we are flying in the face of numerous Scriptures in which He has put His character and His name on the line. He has said, "You can trust me. I will provide."

If we can take God at His Word for personal salvation, for our personal help and protection, why not trust Him in this realm as well?

If you are on the move toward eternity, remember that you are always moving toward your treasure. If your treasure is in eternity, you are always moving toward your treasure. If your treasure is here, you are always moving away from it. If you are on your way to something important, you will understand that it doesn't make any difference if you travel a little lighter down here. The goal and joy of investing in eternity is awaiting you some day in the near future.

APPLICATION

1. Read Nehemiah 1:1–11 and answer the following:

   a. What was the concern of Nehemiah's heart?

   b. What report was he given?

   c. What was his first response?

   d. How did he put his concern into action?

e. What do you think were the key components of his prayer?

2. Now read Nehemiah 2:1–10. What was Nehemiah's next step after prayer?

a. How did his job come into play?

b. What did he do before he spoke?

c. How did God provide for him in light of that?

d. How many different, significant things did God specifically provide, and what were they?

3. Read Deuteronomy 24:19. What did God ask of those whose fields He had blessed?

a. What does God promise to do for those who obey Him in this?

b. Can you think of a godly example of this practice in the Old Testament (see Ruth 2:1–4)?

c. Did God apparently honor His promise?

4. What "harvest," according to Matthew 9:37–38, is most important to God?

a. In what ways might that be relevant to the giving of our "firstfruits"?

5. Read Luke 12:16–21, and answer the following:

   a. How does this man's attitude differ from the one God's Word says we should have?

   b. What was his logic? How was it flawed?

   c. What does God call him? Why?

   d. How might this motivate us to do otherwise? In what way(s)?

6. Read Genesis 14.

   a. What two extremes of attitude toward riches did Abraham display to the king of Sodom and the king of Salem?

   b. Why do you think he refused the gift offered him by the king of Sodom?

   c. Why do you think he then gave a tithe of all to the king of Salem?

   d. What does this passage reveal about setting priorities concerning our material assets?

e. Based on your knowledge about the fate of Sodom and the future of Abraham, what does it reveal about the relationship of God's blessing to wealth and what we do with it?

DID YOU KNOW?

In the episode of Lot's rescue by Abraham, the wealth left behind by the kings of Mesopotamia can only be guessed in light of the level of their panic. A study of the chapter reveals that before they had attacked the kings of the Valley of Siddim, they had been careful to defeat every military force that could launch a counterattack against them. That means when they were attacked at night afterward by Abraham and his servants, in their minds there was only one military force behind them that it could be: Egypt! Fearing for their lives to a man, they would have left behind literally everything not on their backs or in their hands.

This means the wealth offered to Abraham by the king of Sodom would have been immense—which was of no consequence to Abraham in light of his eternal priorities.

THE FAITH OF COMMITMENT

Hebrews 11

This lesson both answers and illustrates the question, "What is the faith of commitment, and what does it look like?"

OUTLINE

In order to understand what the faith of commitment really is, we will examine what it is not as well as what it is. Then we will examine the way it takes shape in our lives.

I. **What the Faith of Commitment Is Not**
   A. It Is Not Blind Optimism
   B. It Is Not Believing in Spite of Evidence
   C. It Is Not the Faith in Faith

II. **What the Faith of Commitment Is**
   A. It Is Initiated by Revelation From God
   B. It Is Ignited by Our Response to Their Revelation
   C. It Is Intensified by the Resistance That It Faces
   D. It Is Inspired by the Reward It Anticipates

III. **Why the Faith of Commitment Works**

W hat is the faith of commitment? Stewardship has a long-lasting benefit for all of us as we review our priorities, as we are brought face to face with almighty God, and as we determine by the grace of God what we will do as individuals and as families in giving to God.

Making a decision by faith about the unknown future is at the very core of the Christian experience. When we make a commitment to God concerning stewardship, we are doing something that is so faith-related that we see God more clearly than in almost any other spiritual activity.

When we come to Christ as sinners and receive His forgiveness, we have made a commitment of faith. We have trusted a God we have not seen and cannot see. Instead, we have read about Him in a book that was written over a period of fourteen hundred years by men and women we have never met. The Bible tells the story of a Savior who lived, died, and was resurrected before any of us were born. Because the Holy Spirit takes the Word of God and makes it real in our hearts, we believe and make a commitment of faith. We call that "conversion."

But from that moment on we also continue to make that same kind of commitment of faith on a daily basis. Moment by moment we trust God, believing Him and putting our future into His loving hands.

Some people have a difficult time making a financial commitment to a church or ministry on the basis of faith alone. But committing ourselves to God by faith is at the very core of who we are as God's people. We do not live and walk by sight. We live and we walk by faith.

In the book of Hebrews we are introduced to some of the great heroes of the past who walked with God. Their names and their accomplishments will never be forgotten because they lived by faith. This chapter is not about a lot of great men and women who did God a favor by doing great things; it is about common, ordinary people who trusted God by faith. Through His strength these people were able to do what they did.

So, what does it mean to express your faith in a commitment to God as those believers did who are memorialized for us in Hebrews 11? First, let's examine what a faith commitment is not.

What the Faith of Commitment Is Not

It Is Not Blind Optimism

A faith of commitment of faith is not just trusting God in the dark, or jumping off a cliff with nowhere to land. A faith commitment is not saying, "I don't understand any of this; it doesn't make any sense to me, but I am just going to trust God."

Some people confuse blind optimism with faith—but commitment faith is not blind optimism.

It Is Not a Believer in Spite of the Evidence

Believing in spite of actual evidence is not faith. That's the exact opposite of faith. Faith is believing because there is evidence.

It Is Not the Faith in Faith

Some people have faith in faith. The real issue of faith is not how much faith you have, but who your faith is in. So again we might ask, what is the faith of commitment?

Having looked at what it is *not*, let's look at what it is.

What the Faith of Commitment Is

It Is Initiated by Revelation From God

God has said something and, because of that, faith comes into play. Romans 10:17 says, "So then, faith comes by hearing, and hearing by the word of God." Faith begins when God speaks. Until God speaks, there isn't anything about faith by itself that is of any value to believers. In every case where the men and women of Hebrews 11 exercised faith, it was in response to something God had told them to do.

Notice Hebrews 11:7: "By faith, Noah, being divinely warned of things not yet seen, moved with godly fear, prepared an ark for the saving of his household."

The reason Noah did what he did was because God spoke to him. His faith was his response to what God said. In other words, the faith of commitment is initiated by revelation.

It Is Ignited by a Response to That Revelation

Faith is not just a matter of saying, "Okay, we believe that." The Bible says the devil believes and trembles. Does that mean he has "saving faith" in God? No. That is mental assent, not faith. Faith is obedience to what God has said. When a person believes God, he does something.

For instance, in Hebrews 11 we are told that Abel *offered* a sacrifice. Noah *prepared* an ark. Abraham *offered* up Isaac. Moses *left* Egypt. When God said, "Do this," they did it. Faith is doing what God says for you to do.

It Is Intensified by the Resistance That It Faces

Every time we take a step of faith, somewhere along the way it will be tested. We see this everywhere in the eleventh chapter of Hebrews. Abraham arrived in the Promised Land, and he walked into a famine. Imagine the abuse Noah put up with from his neighbors after he started building the ark, which took him 120 years to complete. And what about Abraham and Sarah, who—when they are almost a hundred years old—start telling their friends they're going to have a baby.

Someone may say to you, "You actually give ten percent of your income to the Lord? You've got to be nuts!" Not everyone is going to encourage you. When you take your step of faith and begin to walk by faith, be prepared for the fact that your faith will be tested. But know, too, that whenever it is tested, it will get stronger. Testing strengthens faith.

It Is Inspired by the Reward It Anticipates

Notice Hebrews 11:6: "But without faith it is impossible to please Him, for he who comes to God must believe that He is, and that He is a rewarder of those who diligently seek Him."

When we walk by faith, we are looking out into the future beyond the present—we are making an investment for eternity. We are sending some money that we can't keep here to the next land.

WHY THE FAITH OF COMMITMENT WORKS

Two things are eternal: the Word of God, and the souls of men and women. When you invest in those eternal values, that investment is there for eternity.

In Hebrews 11:10, we are told that Abraham "waited for a city whose builder and maker is God." Why? Hebrews 11:16 says it was because "they desire a better, that is, a heavenly country." In other words, they were making their investment now—believing God was going to reward them in the future.

What does God tell us about stewardship, about why the faith of commitment works? Consider these passages:

Malachi 3:10: "'Bring all the tithes into the storehouse, that there may be food in My house, and try Me now in this,' says the Lord of Hosts."

Proverbs 3:9: "Honor the Lord with your possessions, and with the firstfruits of all your increase."

Second Corinthians 9:7: "So let each one give as he purposes in his heart, not grudgingly or of necessity; for God loves a cheerful giver."

And Galatians 6:6–7: "Let him who is taught the word share in all good things with him who teaches. Do not be deceived, God is not mocked; for whatever a man sows, that he will also reap."

Do we have revelation from God about the issue of giving? And is it optional? Quite obviously, we have revelation from God, and tithing is not optional if one is going to be obedient to God. It is not something that some Christians do because they are advanced in their faith. God hasn't changed His mind. He hasn't rewritten a new chapter for this generation. This is the clear revelation we have from Him.

Now, what should our response be?

Deuteronomy 16:17 says, "Every man shall give as he is able."

In 1 Corinthians 16:2 we read, "On the first day of the week let each one of you lay something aside, storing up as he may prosper, that there be no collections when I come."

Hebrews 13:16 says, "But do not forget to do good and to share, for with such sacrifices God is well pleased."

What has God said to us? We are going to make a faith commitment.

But once we have heard God speak, how are we going to respond? A faith commitment is simply a response to what God has said. Am I going to do it? Am I going to do what God has said?

There will always be resistance along the way as you give and as you grow in giving. There will be times when you look around and think about different ways around it. But Galatians 6:9 says, "And let us not grow weary while doing good, for in due season we shall reap if we do not lose heart."

That promise anticipates there will be some tough times when it will be hard to follow through on our commitment of faith. But it's when tough times and resistance come that you break through the resistance and say, "This is God's money—and I am going to give it to Him. By faith I am going to trust Him."

The wonderful news is that there is great reward for good stewardship. What has God promised? Consider these passages:

Proverbs 3:9–10: "Honor the Lord with your possessions, and with the firstfruits of all your increase; so your barns will be filled with plenty, and your vats will overflow with new wine."

Malachi 3:10: "'Bring all the tithes into the storehouse . . . and try Me now in this,' says the Lord of hosts, 'If I will not open for you the windows of heaven and pour out for you such blessing that there will not be room enough to receive it.'"

Luke 6:38: "Give, and it will be given to you: good measure, pressed down, shaken together, and running over will be put into your bosom. For with the same measure that you use, it will be measured back to you."

Second Corinthians 9:6: "But this I say: He who sows sparingly will also reap sparingly, and he who sows bountifully will also reap bountifully."

Second Corinthians 9:8: "And God is able to make all grace abound toward you, that you, always having all sufficiency in all things, may have an abundance for every good work."

Ephesians 6:8: "Knowing that whatever good anyone does, he will receive the same from the Lord, whether he is a slave or free."

And Philippians 4:19: "And my God shall supply all your need according to His riches in glory by Christ Jesus."

We have a reward—so what do we do? God has spoken, and we know what He has said. God has spoken, and He has put it in simple terms.

Now, our response is going to be either to say, "Okay, Lord, I am going to do what You said," or not to do what He says. When we do what He says, we may face a little challenge along the way. But we will steer right through it and not be weary in well-doing. We see the reward, that God is going to bless those who honor Him in such a way. Notice what Hebrews 12:1–3 says:

> Therefore we also, since we are surrounded by so great a cloud of witnesses, let us lay aside every weight, and the sin which so easily ensnares us, and let us run with endurance the race that is set before us, looking unto Jesus, the author and finisher of our faith, who for the joy that was set before Him endured the cross, despising the shame, and has sat down at the right hand of the throne of God. For consider Him who endured such hostility from sinners against Himself, lest you become weary and discouraged in your souls.

We have a great example in our Lord, just as we have a great example in these men and women who lived by faith. God is asking us to take a simple little step of faith and say, "Through Your grace Lord, I am going to begin giving back to You ten percent of everything You entrust to me. I am going to listen to You and respond to what You have said. And then I am going to trust You to provide."

That, my friend, is what it means to walk by faith.

APPLICATION

1. Examine the following passages and then comment on the ways each biblical character put his or her commitment of faith into action:

   1 Samuel 1:11, 27–28

   Genesis 12:1; 14:18–20

   2 Samuel 24:21–24

2. List at least five objections you might hear from unbelievers concerning the practice of giving a tenth of everything to God. If possible, after each briefly state what your answer to them would be.

   1.

   2.

   3.

   4.

   5.

3. Read Malachi 3:8–10 and consider:

   a. For what offense does God accuse Israel?

   b. What is their anticipated response to His accusation (verse 8b)?

   c. What is the consequence of this offense against God?

   d. What alternative does God offer them?

e. Why do you think Israel should not have hesitated to give God His tithe?

f. Why do you think they did hesitate?

g. How would you summarize the relationship between obedience and blessing in this passage?

4. Malachi 3:8–10 is actually God's answer to a problem and question found in Malachi 3:7. In light of that, what was the real problem?

a. What was God's desire in relation to that problem?

b. What was Israel's anticipated question in that regard?

5. Based on Malachi 3, what is the connection between God's revelation and Israel's obedience in giving Him His tithe?

a. What would the connection be for believers?

DID YOU KNOW?

History tells us that the "tithe" given to a conquering military commander in ancient times was not merely a tenth of the spoils; it was "the tenth off the top." Following a conquest, all the treasure confiscated from the enemy was stacked for review by the commander and his army, with the most valuable goods placed at the top of the stack. After it was examined, pay to the soldiers would be distributed from it. However, the first to get his due was the commander, who was—out of gratitude from his army—given the top tenth of the stack. In other words, he was given the choicest of the spoils, which often would be more valuable than all the rest of the treasure combined. Why? Because his army knew that apart from him, they would have nothing.

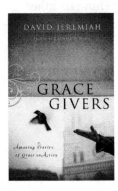

The Grace of Giving

Financial stewardship can turn into a rote chore if you don't understand the grace of giving. In this series, Dr. Jeremiah introduces you to one aspect of your Christian life that can revolutionize your faith. *The Grace of Giving* series will cause you to investigate your priorities, obedience, and motives in light of God's blessings and provision. Available in study guide or CD album format.

Investing for Eternity

Money. It can be the cause of wars, divorces, and the demise of friendships. But money is also the resource that sends the Gospel into local communities and around the world. In this series Dr. Jeremiah provides answers from the Scriptures for perhaps the most difficult subject of our times— investing for eternity. Available in study guide or CD album format.

Each of these books was created from a teaching series by Dr. David Jeremiah. Each series is also available with correlating study guides and CD audio albums.

For pricing information and ordering, contact us at www.DavidJeremiah.org or call (800) 947-1993.

STAY CONNECTED
TO DR. DAVID JEREMIAH

Take advantage of two great ways to let Dr. David Jeremiah give you
spiritual direction every day! Both are absolutely FREE.

Turning Points Magazine and Devotional

Receive Dr. David Jeremiah's monthly
magazine, *Turning Points* each month:

- Monthly study focus
- 52 pages of life-changing reading
- Relevant articles
- Special features
- Humor section
- Family section
- Daily devotional readings for each
  day of the month
- Bible study resource offers
- Live event schedule
- Radio & television information

Your Daily Turning Point E-Devotional

Start your day off right! Find words of inspiration
and spiritual motivation waiting for you on your
computer every morning! You can receive a daily
e-devotional communication from David Jeremiah
that will strengthen your walk with God and
encourage you to live the authentic Christian life.

There are two easy ways to sign up for these free resources from
Turning Point. Visit us online at www.DavidJeremiah.org and select
"Subscribe to *Turning Points* Magazine" or visit the home page and find
Daily Devotional to subscribe to your daily e-devotional.